The Tudors: A Very Short Introduction

VERY SHORT INTRODUCTIONS are for anyone wanting a stimulating and accessible way into a new subject. They are written by experts, and have been translated into more than 45 different languages.

The series began in 1995, and now covers a wide variety of topics in every discipline. The VSI library now contains over 500 volumes—a Very Short Introduction to everything from Psychology and Philosophy of Science to American History and Relativity—and continues to grow in every subject area.

Titles in the series include the following:

John Guy

THE TUDORS

A Very Short Introduction

OXFORD
UNIVERSITY PRESS

OXFORD
UNIVERSITY PRESS

Great Clarendon Street, Oxford, OX2 6DP,
United Kingdom

Oxford University Press is a department of the University of Oxford.
It furthers the University's objective of excellence in research, scholarship,
and education by publishing worldwide. Oxford is a registered trade mark of
Oxford University Press in the UK and in certain other countries

Text first published in *The Oxford Illustrated History of Britain* 1984
Revised text © John Guy 2000
Second edition text © John Guy 2013

The moral rights of the author have been asserted

Second Edition published in 2013

Impression: 13

Published in the United States of America by Oxford University Press
198 Madison Avenue, New York, NY 10016, United States of America

British Library Cataloguing in Publication Data
Data available

ISBN 978-0-19-967472-5

Printed and bound by CPI Group (UK) Ltd, Croydon, CR0 4YY

Contents

List of illustrations

Genealogical table

THE TUDOR SUCCESSION

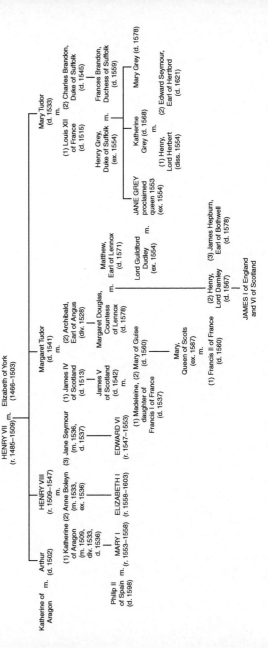

Note on units of currency

In citing units of currency, the old sterling denominations of pounds, shillings, and pence have been retained. There are 12 pence (12d.) in a shilling (modern 5 pence or US 8 cents), 20 shillings (20s.) in a pound (£1 or US$1.60), and so on. A mark is 13s. 4d. (66 pence or US$1.05). Rough estimates of modern values for 16th-century figures can be obtained by multiplying all the numbers by 1,000.

Chapter 1
Henry VII: Founding a new dynasty

Winning the throne

On the morning of Monday, 22 August 1485, Henry, Earl of Richmond, a tall, slender 28-year-old with blue eyes and thick brown hair, a man with a will of steel and a terrifying urge to power, won the throne of England in a fierce battle fought not far from Market Bosworth in Leicestershire. After initial exchanges of gunfire and arrows, the crack troops of Henry's vanguard attacked the larger forces of the 32-year-old King Richard III on their right wing and with the sun behind them. A counter-attack was repulsed, and as the battle began to turn against him, Richard gambled on a victory by charging forward in a bold attempt to kill Henry, who stood with a small retinue towards the rear of his army.

In full armour and wearing his gold battle crown and surcoat of the royal arms, Richard galloped around the site of the main battle at the head of his heavily armed household knights to encircle his rival. Stopped in his tracks by a solid wall of Swiss-trained pikemen who dropped back in a tight formation from Henry's vanguard at the last moment, Richard dismounted and began to fight hand-to-hand. At this point Sir William Stanley—Henry's step-uncle, who thus far had been shadowing the rival armies without committing himself—threw his forces into the battle on Henry's side. Cut off from reinforcements, Richard clawed his way through the wall of pikemen and engaged Henry's bodyguards in mortal combat. He reached his rival's standard-bearer and cut him down, but was overpowered and bludgeoned to death, after which his battle crown was hacked from his helmet and placed on Henry's head.

Henry marched into Leicester and then slowly on towards London, which he entered in triumph on 3 September. Richard's naked corpse was slung on the back of a horse and paraded before the crowds in Leicester, then hastily buried at the Franciscan friary called the Grey Friars.

Henry had made his own luck, for when he was born, his father, Edmund, Earl of Richmond, King Henry VI's half-brother, was already dead. His claim to the throne came largely through his redoubtable mother, Lady Margaret Beaufort, the only daughter of John Beaufort, Duke of Somerset, and a great-great-granddaughter of King Edward III through the liaison of John of Gaunt, Duke of Lancaster, with his long-standing mistress Katherine Swynford. But in 1407, King Henry IV, the first Lancastrian king, had specifically barred the Beaufort line from the succession, so the young Earl of Richmond's claim was weak.

Henry's victory at Bosworth was the culmination of some 30 or so years of dynastic strife and civil wars that had followed Henry VI's mental breakdown in 1453. An attempt by Richard, Duke of York, to capture the throne in 1460 had failed and York was slain six months later at the battle of Wakefield. But his son Edward succeeded where his father failed, winning the battle of Towton in 1461. At the age of 18, Edward deposed Henry VI and took the throne as King Edward IV, holding his position more or less unchallenged until 1483—apart from in 1470–1, when Henry VI was briefly restored.

When Edward died in April 1483, he was succeeded by the elder of his surviving sons, the 12-year-old Edward V, but in June the boy was deposed by his uncle, Richard, Duke of Gloucester, who was crowned as Richard III. Gloucester's usurpation re-ignited the civil wars, also provoking what was strongly rumoured to be the murders in the Tower of London of Edward V and his younger brother Richard—the boys disappeared suddenly, even if the mystery of how exactly they died, who killed them, and how their bodies were disposed of has never been completely solved. As opinion turned against Gloucester, an underground network of those who feared or hated him offered their support to the young Henry, Earl of Richmond, an exile in Brittany and France since 1471.

Margaret Beaufort was among those plotting against Richard, conspiring with Elizabeth Woodville, Edward IV's widow, to agree that if Henry secured the throne, he would quickly marry Woodville's daughter, Elizabeth of York, who was the chief hope of the surviving Yorkists. And the promise was honoured, for less than six weeks after Henry was crowned and his title to the throne confirmed by act of Parliament, he asked Elizabeth to marry him and the nuptials took place in January 1486.

The problem of security

At first, Henry (Figure 1) was a highly effective ruler, who restored a stable monarchy and took several of Edward IV's trusted councillors into his service, although he rarely allowed them to take precedence over his fellow-exiles or his mother's key advisers, who dominated his inner circle. Elizabeth of York proved herself to be a talented peacemaker, even if she tended to be overshadowed by her overbearing mother-in-law, who styled herself 'Margaret R' as if she and not Elizabeth were queen.

For many former Yorkists, however, the new king was a usurper with the weakest of dynastic credentials. Sullen compliance from such men did not mean acceptance and the problem of security would trouble Henry for much of his reign. Some of his fears were justified, but others were not, being a result of the darker

1. Henry VII as he approached the age of 50, an image in which the artist captures some aspects of the darker side of his character

side of his character, for he was deeply suspicious of all those around him and, despite his love of tennis, gambling, archery, and above all hunting and hawking, he could be distant and reclusive, often withdrawing into his Privy Chamber with a few close intimates, and slipping in and out of his palaces by the back door.

Had Henry been more trusting, it is possible he would not have been troubled by plots and rebellions for as long as he was. But he faced a dilemma—as a contemporary remarked, 'Hard is it to know men's minds if God should send a sudden change, as he hath heretofore'. No one could be sure which way the nobles or leading courtiers would jump in a fresh crisis. On the face of it, Henry was lucky in that—unlike Edward IV, who had begun his reign with his predecessor not just alive but still at large—his rival Richard III was dead, as were so many of the old Yorkist nobles and knights, and there was no obvious cadet (i.e., descended from a younger son) branch of the royal family.

Henry was especially fortunate that Elizabeth of York was fecund. She conceived with relative ease, and four of her children, Arthur (b. 1486), Margaret (b. 1489), Henry (b. 1491), and Mary (b. 1496), survived into their teenage years or beyond, even if others died young or in infancy. Whether the queen's fecundity alone could ensure the new dynasty's survival was far from clear, but as an immediate precaution, Henry put the Yorkist with the strongest claim to the throne, Edward, Earl of Warwick—the eldest and only living son of Edward IV's brother, George, Duke of Clarence—in the Tower.

Of the leading conspirators and pretenders who dogged Henry in the first 12 years of his reign, Lambert Simnel was the easiest to deal with, even though he (or rather his powerful backers) posed a serious threat thanks to widespread support in Ireland and Yorkshire. Described as 'a comely youth', Simnel was something of a chameleon, first posing as Richard, Duke of York, which was plausible as their ages were the same, and then the Earl of Warwick. His backers included John de la Pole, Earl of Lincoln, a nephew of Edward IV who had fought for Richard III at Bosworth, and Margaret of York, the Dowager Duchess of Burgundy, Edward's youngest sister and the only one to make a foreign marriage. The young imposter's forces included 2,000 German mercenaries supplied by Margaret and 4,000 Irish foot soldiers, but Henry routed them at the battle of Stoke (16 June 1487). Those of Simnel's supporters who were not killed fighting like the Earl of Lincoln either fled into exile or were pardoned. Simnel himself was captured and taken into the king's household as a servant, where he worked in the scullery before rising to become a falconer.

Fresh plots and revolts in Yorkshire in 1489 and 1491 led to a series of executions, the imposition of large fines, or the flight of the conspirators into exile. Henry had few friends north of the River Trent—the region from which Richard III had drawn most of his support—and many lords and gentry there were still keen to harness local grievances to Yorkist ends. Until 1500 or so, Henry had only fitful control of the North, where a regional rising, supported by an invasion from Scotland, seemed all too plausible.

Increasingly dangerous was a conspiracy nurtured in Ireland in the later months of 1491 that put forward a second pretender, the teenager Perkin Warbeck. A youth considered to have a striking physical resemblance to Richard, Duke of York, Warbeck was brought up in Tournai, where he had modelled silks for Flemish cloth merchants trading mainly in Portugal and Ireland before his backers moved him to the safety of the Court of King Charles VIII of France in March 1492. The news of his arrival there obliged Henry to begin preparations for a full-scale war against France.

A vast English army crossed the Channel, but Henry proved how his natural guile and skilful diplomacy could often achieve peace and neutralize the Yorkist cause's foreign allies without any actual fighting. After making a show of strength for a month and reasserting Henry V's claim to the French crown, his aim was to make a quick treaty—a move in which Charles VIII connived. Eager to cross the Alps and invade Italy, the French king agreed to drop his support for Warbeck and other Yorkist claimants and to indemnify Henry's costs in full.

Warbeck escaped to Malines in the Burgundian Netherlands, where Margaret of York welcomed him as her long-lost nephew. Five anxious years followed in which Henry had to deal with plots and revolts, real and imagined, in Ireland (especially) and northern England. And on the Continent, he was boxed into unceasing negotiations and a costly trade war affecting wool and cloth exports to the Netherlands while Warbeck travelled around collecting fresh backers. By 1495, Warbeck had even sensationally won over the same Sir William Stanley—now the king's chamberlain of the household—who had so decisively intervened on Henry's side at the battle of Bosworth. When Sir William's treasonable correspondence with Warbeck was exposed and he was beheaded, shockwaves ran through Henry's Court, since it was plain that Yorkist conspiracy had penetrated deep into the king's inner circle.

A crisis was set in train when Warbeck, having botched an invasion of England in the summer of 1495, arrived in Scotland, where King James IV welcomed him and married him in January 1496 to Lady Katherine Gordon, daughter of George, Earl of Huntly. James gave Warbeck and his 1,400 followers Falkland Palace as a home, from where the pretender began to plan an invasion of England. The following September, James and Warbeck crossed the frontier, hoping to raise the whole of the North in rebellion. But the raid misfired and James, to whom Warbeck had promised the border town of Berwick, was left to demolish a few towers and burn down crops and houses. Henry, however, believed that this was merely the prelude to a test of his kingship and set about mustering another battle army, this time to invade Scotland.

It was Henry's taxation for the imminent war that triggered a mass revolt in Cornwall. The inhabitants—who had a strong sense of regional identity and many of whom, in the area west of Truro, still spoke Cornish—refused to pay a tax for a campaign in Scotland for which they believed a land tax levied in the northern shires alone was the correct source of finance. Led by a blacksmith from St Keverne on the Lizard and by the son of one of the king's own tax commissioners, a large army of rebels set off in May 1497 to march to London. In Somerset they were joined by a disaffected noble, Lord Audley, and by the time they camped on Blackheath, near Greenwich, they were more than 15,000 strong.

No sooner had Henry's forces defeated the rebels and hanged or beheaded the ringleaders than the king turned to Scotland. Once again, luck was on his side—in August that year he was able to make a truce with James IV, to last for seven years, at Ayton in Cleveland. By the terms of the accord James abandoned his claim to Berwick and agreed to revoke the safe-conduct he had granted to Henry's rebels since 1495. More to the point, he expelled them from his realm and agreed to terms binding each of the two rulers not to harbour each other's rebels. Furthermore, it was agreed that, when the truce expired, James would marry Henry's eldest daughter, Margaret, thereby cementing the truce into what at the time was called a Treaty of Perpetual Peace.

Barely had Henry time to breathe before Warbeck's forces landed in Cornwall in September 1497, and a fresh revolt began. When he disembarked, Warbeck had barely 300 supporters, but by the time they laid siege to Exeter they had been joined by the remnants of the rebel forces from Blackheath and were said to be 8,000 strong. Troops led by the Earl of Devon withstood the siege, and the invaders withdrew to Taunton. As Henry's forces, many of them mustered to fight in Scotland, marched at full speed towards them, the rebels began to melt away. Warbeck fled, but was soon captured and paraded through the streets of London as an imposter. Locked up by Henry, he escaped but was recaptured. He was finally hanged in November 1499 after he and two accomplices plotted to free both himself and the real Earl of Warwick from their cells in the Tower and to place one of them on the throne. At this point, Warbeck's escape plot was made the pretext for beheading the Earl, who was put on trial for conspiring to depose Henry.

There was, however, a more pressing reason why Warwick had to die. In 1488, Henry, who was keen to secure a dynastic alliance

The Tudors

with one of the strongest powers in Europe, had begun negotiations with King Ferdinand of Aragon and his wife Isabella of Castile designed to betroth their youngest daughter, Katherine, to Prince Arthur. By the Treaty of Medina del Campo (1489) Ferdinand and Isabella had closed Spain to Yorkist pretenders and a future marriage alliance was settled in principle. The young couple were then married by proxy (though this was not considered to be binding) in May 1499, when a final agreement was reached on a substantial dowry. Ferdinand and Isabella agreed that Katherine would be sent to England when Arthur was 14. However, the Spanish monarchs, besides haggling over the enormous dowry demanded by Henry, were anxious about the threat to Henry's regime from Yorkist plots, and the diplomatic evidence suggests that it was their concerns that led to Warwick's trial and execution.

Even before Warwick was beheaded, Edmund de la Pole, Earl of Suffolk, a younger brother of the rebel Earl of Lincoln and the next in line as a convincing Yorkist claimant, came to fear for his life. Being loyal to Henry, Suffolk had ignored Lord Bergavenny's suggestion that they both join Lord Audley and the Cornish rebels, and he had removed Bergavenny's shoes at a crucial moment so as to immobilize him. But as a punishment for Lincoln's treachery, Henry placed draconian conditions on Suffolk's rights of inheritance and in July 1499 the Earl travelled, without licence, first to Guisnes, one of the flanking fortresses of the last English outpost in France at Calais, and then to St Omer in Flanders, seeking the protection of his aunt, Margaret of York. His friends, among them Sir James Tyrell, a member of Henry's garrison at Calais, entertained him and secretly offered him help should he wish to defect permanently.

Suffolk was persuaded to return, and heavily fined, but two years later he fled for good with his brother Richard to Aachen, where he began to plot a Yorkist invasion of England. Henry struck back, mobilizing a web of spies and informers to infiltrate Suffolk's retinue. He rounded up and imprisoned at the Tower or the castle at Calais most of the surviving males with a Yorkist connection. In a purge lasting four years between 1502 and 1506, the Earl's supporters were interrogated, Sir James Tyrell was beheaded, and Suffolk and his retinue were declared by the courts to be outlaws with a bounty on their heads.

Meanwhile, Katherine of Aragon had arrived in England, and she and Arthur were married at Old St Paul's Cathedral on 14 November 1501. Arthur, who at the age of 3 had been invested as Prince of Wales in a splendid ceremony in the Parliament Chamber at Westminster, was now 15. It was decided that he and Katherine, who was almost a year older, should travel to his princely capital of Ludlow on the borders of Wales and live there together in the royal apartments at the castle as man and wife. This was at the zenith of Henry's reign, the point at which, for the first time since he had captured the crown, he had almost everything within his control. With Arthur and Katherine married and living together, a grandson for Henry might now also be expected. With the exception of the problem of Edmund and Richard de la Pole, who paradoxically rose higher on the king's radar even as he marginalized and impoverished them by his intensively active diplomacy, it looked as if the Tudor dynasty had a secure future.

Creating a new monarchy

A hands-on ruler for whom no detail was too small, Henry checked the most important accounts of his receipts and expenditure personally, often signing them on every page. Dedicated and attentive, astute and ascetic, his view of the need for a more interventionist and centralized government was modelled less on traditional English values and more on those of Brittany and France, where he had been in exile.

His mantra was enforcement—the enforcement of political and financial obligation to the king, as much as of law and order after the civil wars. In restoring the power of the monarchy, he held that ability, good service, and loyalty to the regime, rather than noble birth, were to be the essential qualifications for appointments, patronage, and rewards. Whereas the Yorkist kings had been content to partner the nobility in government, Henry's goal was a monarchy in which the nobles served the king. Only veteran Lancastrian peers such as John de Vere, Earl of Oxford, could count themselves safe. To subordinate the nobles, Henry subverted their territorial influence, heavily fining them simply for taking up their inheritances when they succeeded to their estates, closely vetting which of them should continue to be appointed as local magistrates, and undercutting their authority wherever he could by taking their leading gentry supporters into his own household.

Henry's key advisers at the time he won the throne were men who had either been with him in exile or were introduced to him by his mother, notably Cardinal John Morton, Richard Fox, Giles Daubeney, and Sir Reynold Bray. Others, like John, Lord Dynham, had been loyal servants of Edward IV who had switched their allegiance. Of those Henry appointed in the months and years after his coronation, he preferred ambitious middling gentry and sharp-eyed lawyers such as Sir Thomas Lovell, Sir Henry Wyatt, and later (and most notoriously) Richard Empson and Edmund Dudley. Progressively, he turned them into a distinctive cadre of 'new men', whom Perkin Warbeck (attempting to win noble support) disparaged as 'caitiffs and villeins [i.e., base wretches and scoundrels] of simple birth whom the king alone trusted'.

Bray, for instance, was a former estate officer for Margaret Beaufort and a surgeon's son. Ably supported by Lovell (as Treasurer of the King's Chamber) and Wyatt (as Master of the King's Jewels), whose fathers were minor gentry, he established himself as Henry's chief financial controller and enforcer of his rights, using a much-feared tribunal known as the Council Learned in the Law. When Bray died in 1503, Empson, said to be a sieve-maker's son and a brilliant lawyer, succeeded him, partnered by Dudley, another scion of a lesser gentry family and a star of the legal profession who rose to be Speaker of the House of Commons.

Such men exercised control, under the king, far in excess of their apparent status. For, in a surprisingly short space of time, Henry managed to devise a novel mesh of interlocking fiscal and administrative checks and blueprints, the records of which never left his own hands or those of the chosen few. These dealt with financial accounting, the exploitation of the undervalued resources of the crown lands, the collection of debts and fines, and the enforcement of Henry's punitive system of forcing political opponents—or even apparent friends—to enter into coercive bonds for future conduct such as allegiance, appearance before a court of law, or good 'abearing' (i.e., behaviour). In overseeing these myriad functions, Henry's 'new men' proved themselves to be dedicated agents of royal power: meritocratic, focused, efficient, and as potentially unscrupulous and as quick to pick up on treason as the king himself.

A series of calamities

Just when it seemed in the closing months of 1501 that the new dynasty was secured, a series of sudden blows stunned Henry. His troubles began in early February 1502, when Prince Arthur, his heir and the dynasty's hope, fell sick at Ludlow Castle. After 27 March, his condition rapidly worsened until, on 2 April, he died from an unknown cause, which from the inadequately recorded symptoms may have been plague, tuberculosis, or testicular cancer.

Attempting to comfort him, Elizabeth of York reminded Henry that they had a healthy second son and two daughters, and could try for another child. Sure enough, Elizabeth was soon pregnant again. On 2 February 1503, she was successfully delivered of a daughter, but she never recovered from her labour and died on the morning of her 37th birthday. Her baby also died.

With his wife and the Prince of Wales gone, Henry became more haunted than ever before by fears of plots and pretenders. He retreated into his Privy Chamber, where he put a ring of steel around himself, tormented by anxiety for his dynasty's survival and over-protective of his younger son, Henry, Duke of York, whom he now rarely allowed out of his sight.

Always fearful to the point of obsession of Yorkist plots, Henry increasingly sought out information from spies and informers. His health, meanwhile, started to fail. His hair went white and he had increasing difficulties with his eyesight. He suffered a minor stroke and afterwards found writing difficult. After he had lain sick for several weeks at Wanstead, it was reported at Calais that 'the king's grace is but a weak man and sickly, not likely to be no long lived man'. According to one of his spies, there was growing speculation 'of the world that should be after him if his grace happened to depart'. Among those canvassed as possible successors if Henry died were Edmund de la Pole and (less predictably) Edward Stafford, Duke of Buckingham, Edward IV's nephew by marriage and the country's richest peer. Buckingham as a child had been a ward of Henry's mother, but now it seemed that 'many great personages' were saying that he 'was a noble man and would be a royal ruler'. What Henry's informant said that most upset the declining king was that none of those who had been overheard gossiping about the succession had mentioned his own younger son.

As Henry's spies flooded him with information after 1503, they created a twilight world of suspicion and fear in which no one felt sure whom they could trust any more. Given the spider's web he was creating, Henry's greatest weakness would be his reluctance to believe the evil reports circulating against his own agents. It was a situation that snowballed as foreign diplomats started to remark that 'those who have received the greatest favours from him are the most suspected'.

And yet, despite his increasing paranoia, Henry never quite lost his grip. When in 1504 Edmund de la Pole, Earl of Suffolk, left Aachen and was imprisoned on his way to Friesland by servants of the Duke of Gueldres, Henry promptly paid Gueldres to detain him until negotiations could be completed with Archduke Philip the Handsome, the ruler of the Netherlands, for his extradition. He then bombarded Philip with gifts and attention—a single payment in the spring of 1505 was a 'loan' of £138,000 (more than his entire annual revenue from the crown lands)—ostensibly to assist with his preparations to take up the throne of Castile, which his wife Juana had inherited after her mother Isabella's death, but in reality to bribe him to extradite Suffolk.

Henry got his way in 1506 when Philip and Juana were accidentally blown ashore near Weymouth on their outward voyage to Spain. Seizing his opportunity, Henry lured Philip inland and royally entertained him at Windsor Castle and Richmond Palace, flattering him with lavish and costly entertainments and showering him with gifts and attention. One result was a trade agreement that was highly favourable to the English merchant guilds. But far more important for Henry, Philip offered—as it was reported 'unasked'—to hand over Suffolk. By then, the unfortunate Earl was in prison at Namur. He was so miserable that he offered to return to England voluntarily and was escorted across the frontier to Calais, from where he was promptly shipped across the Channel to Dover. Met by one of Henry's 'new men', he was taken to London, closely interrogated, and imprisoned in the Tower.

Financial rapacity

Henry became greedy and avaricious in the last years of his reign, increasingly resented for his fiscal extortions and summary approach to justice, not least in London. By then, he was keeping parallel sets of accounts, one an official set and another recording the proceeds of his extortions. The latter included the profits of his illegal involvement in the lucrative alum trade in which he used royal navy ships to smuggle alum from the Ottoman world to London, in defiance of a papal embargo, before re-exporting it to the Netherlands, where it was chiefly used in cloth manufacturing as a dye-fixer. One shipment alone was worth over £15,000 (£15 million in modern values).

A visiting collector of papal taxes—an Italian named Polydore Vergil—wrote a *History of England* in which he claimed that Henry became rapacious after Arthur's death:

> For he began to treat his people with more harshness and severity than had been his custom, in order (as he himself asserted) to ensure that they remained more thoroughly and entirely in obedience to him. The people themselves had another explanation for his action, for they considered they were suffering not on account of their own sins but on account of the greed of their monarch. It is not indeed clear whether at the start it was greed; but afterwards greed did become apparent.

After Empson and Dudley succeeded Bray as the king's financial controllers, the dubious morality of the tactics used was blatant. Whereas Bray had sought credible evidence of disloyalty or infringements of royal rights before taking action, Empson and Dudley used false information or ferreted out evidence of past accusations long ago dismissed by the courts, which was then used to bring prosecutions against law-abiding citizens. The victims either had to pay crippling fines or were forced to enter into coercive bonds for future conduct. Anyone accused again would discover that the penalties of their bonds had automatically been converted into genuine debts to the Crown, bypassing the law.

If that were not enough, when cases did go to court, Empson and Dudley bribed and threatened juries or even chose the jury panels themselves to ensure they got convictions, saying 'all was done in the king's name'. Henry, meanwhile, was selling judicial offices to the highest bidder. Twice he sold the chief justiceship of the Court of Common Pleas, and at high prices. He also sold the posts of Attorney-General, Master of the Rolls, and Speaker of the House of Commons.

Using a deadly combination of surveillance, blackmail, intimidation, and extortion, Empson and Dudley ruthlessly cowed opposition even where it did not exist. Contemporaries, as under Richard III, called such methods 'exquisite means' (i.e., ingenious methods of decidedly dubious legality). Many of Henry's subjects, even if they had been loyal up to 1503, would turn against him in the last years of the reign. The result was a backlash—the reopening of dynastic wounds. 'Change of worlds hath caused change of mind' was an aphorism one of the king's informers told him was circulating among the garrison at Calais. And the mood of fear and uncertainty was clearly felt at Court, where rumours of corruption and of old Yorkist ties brought fines, imprisonment, or disgrace to peers already on Henry's lists of suspects, such as Lord Bergavenny and Thomas Grey, Marquis of Dorset.

As it turned out, Henry did successfully pass on his throne to his surviving son, but not automatically. His death at around 11 pm on Saturday, 21 April 1509, was followed by a Court coup in which his inner courtiers jockeyed, Kremlin-style, for positions in the new reign. Only after a deal had been reached in a secret cabal that Empson and Dudley would be thrown to the wolves to appease the sullen and resentful Londoners was the rest of the Court informed. It was thus not until Tuesday the 24th that the heralds proclaimed the accession of the younger Henry. At the same time, illegally held prisoners were quietly released from the Tower and other prisons.

Henry had died just at the right moment—before someone started using the danger of disaffection as an argument for increasing his own authority as Richard, Duke of Gloucester, had done on the eve of his usurpation in 1483. The need for the king never again to alienate quite so many wealthy landowners and leading London citizens in so short a time as Henry VII had done would be a lesson those in power would remember for a decade or more to come.

Chapter 2

Henry VIII: The personification of power

The earliest years

Henry VIII became king at two months short of 18 years of age. Six feet two inches tall and as lean as he was fit before gluttony caused him to bulge, he longed to be a famous ruler like Alexander the Great and seemed to be everything his subjects expected in a new monarch. That he was easily angered, emotionally predatory, and had a mind that brooded over petty slights were traits unsuspected at his accession.

Always a man of action, Henry was a superb athlete who excelled at jousting, tilting, hunting, and hawking, at archery, wrestling, and tennis. An indefatigable horseman, he liked to ride for miles every day. Imagining himself as a warrior called to imitate the glorious victories in France of Edward III's eldest son the Black Prince and of Henry V during the Hundred Years War, he renewed his father's peace with France in 1509 only under protest. His heart was full of chivalric ardour and martial zeal. Highly competitive in war and peace, he expected to win at whatever he did.

Besides his physical accomplishments, Henry was well-educated and intelligent. A fluent speaker of Latin and French with a smattering of Italian and Spanish, he was able to converse readily

with visiting ambassadors and—despite a limited attention span—
was something of an expert on theology, astronomy, fortifications,
and maps. A talented musician, he could sing at sight and play the
lute and virginals, composing several of his own songs—the opening
lines of one of them sum up his youthful sentiments:

> Pastime with good company
> I love and shall until I die.
> Grudge who will—but none deny—
> So God be pleased, thus live will I.

At the great religious festivals, chiefly Christmas, Epiphany,
Easter, and Whitsuntide, Henry sat in state at one or other of his
palaces wearing his purple robes, flanked by his nobles, bishops,
and leading councillors, before processing in majesty to the
Chapel Royal to hear mass.

The sheer opulence of his Court was extraordinary. When he died,
he possessed over 60 houses, the furnishings of which included some
2,000 tapestries, over 150 panel paintings, and 2,028 pieces of gold
or silver plate. Nine of his larger palaces, mostly in the Thames
Valley between Greenwich and Windsor, were capable of housing
the entire Court for weeks at a time and were kept constantly
furnished. Each had a vast maze of rooms with a great hall, Chapel,
separate apartments for the king and queen, a long gallery, privy
gardens, and lodgings for courtiers, not to mention kitchens, stables,
a laundry, and space for all the other domestic functions (Figure 2).

Following the secret deal reached around his father's deathbed,
Henry began his reign with a series of grand gestures designed to
win him instant popularity, making scapegoats of Empson and
Dudley, who were sent to the Tower and convicted of treason.
In parallel, Henry proclaimed a general pardon of offences
committed by his subjects, including (with certain exceptions)
high treason or felony, and invited anyone with grievances against
the old king or his bureaucrats to report them to his councillors.

2. Something of the opulence of Henry VIII's Court can be glimpsed from this 17th-century copy of the dynastic wall fresco that the king commissioned in *c.*1537 from Hans Holbein the Younger for the Privy Chamber at Whitehall Palace (described in Chapter 7)

Thousands flocked to file their petitions, although very little was ever done to compensate them.

The next thing Henry did was a surprise even to those who had sat around his father's bedside. Armed with a papal bull of dispensation, the teenage king married Katherine of Aragon, his brother Arthur's widow, declaring himself to be deeply in love and sweeping aside objections that she was nearly six years older than he was.

Until 1527 or so, Henry would spend much of his time amusing himself, paying less attention to affairs of state than he would later in life, and preferring to delegate the running of the country to his ministers and councillors. But he retained a close watching brief. His ministers kept him abreast of affairs by correspondence, making visits to Court usually on Sundays. The king's in-letters, from English ambassadors abroad as well as his ministers, were read aloud to him by his secretaries, who drafted replies on lines the king dictated before signature. Henry's right to intervene in any aspect of government when he chose meant that his signature (or 'sign manual') was essential to the running of the country. His councillors and servants competed to get decisions made or documents signed in the course of early morning mass or in the evening after Henry returned from a long day's hunting. Documents could be held in a queue for weeks, and sometimes months, if he refused to sign his name for any reason.

Such personal monarchy could be raw and brutal. In 1521, fearful of the wealth and old Yorkist connections of Edward Stafford, Duke of Buckingham, Henry put the Duke on trial on trumped-up treason charges. Buckingham, he said, was plotting to depose him, and when one of the Duke's disgruntled servants came forward to claim, on the basis of hearsay, that Buckingham had been ready to rebel, Henry moved in for the kill. The Duke protested that his trial was rigged, for Henry interviewed and even coached the witnesses beforehand, forcing information out of Buckingham's chaplain and so breaking the seal of the confessional. It was a defining moment, teaching Henry that, rather than bypassing the law as his father's bureaucrats had sometimes done, he could instead subvert it, getting everything he wanted, apparently legally.

Wolsey's ascendancy

Henry chose Thomas Wolsey, a butcher's son from Ipswich who had climbed his way up the ladder at Oxford and Henry VII's Court, to be his first chief minister. Appointed the new king's almoner and one of his chaplains at the beginning of the reign,

Wolsey came to prominence after Henry's elder and more sober councillors had attempted to rein in his extravagance and prevent him from putting his name to royal gifts or grants without the counter-signature of one or usually two of them. Always determined to exercise an untrammelled royal authority, Henry had rebelled, and since Wolsey had often been sent to explain things to him, he had the opportunity to advise the king in private. It was during one of those conversations that Henry—according to Wolsey's chief gentleman-usher, George Cavendish—found that his almoner 'was the most earnest and readiest among all the Council to advance the king's only will and pleasure without any respect to the case'.

If Cavendish is to be believed, Wolsey had no guiding political principles. He had instead a will to serve the king and to succeed, this combined with 'a special gift of natural eloquence with a filed tongue to pronounce the same, that he was able with the same to persuade and allure all men to his purpose.' If pragmatism was the key to Wolsey's rise, eloquence was the key to his allure: he was the master of 'persuasions'. In the Renaissance (and notably in diplomacy) nothing was more essential. As Castiglione advised in *The Book of the Courtier*, if the courtier were unable to move the minds of others by eloquence and so to persuade princes, nobles, and foreign ambassadors towards a recommended course of action, he would fail. And to persuade, it was necessary to charm and to mould language 'like wax after his own mind'.

No one would be quicker than Wolsey to accumulate offices and power. By 1514, he had made himself indispensable to Henry, who nominated him as bishop of Lincoln, the largest diocese in England. The king then began lobbying the pope to make his chief minister a cardinal. When the archbishopric of York fell unexpectedly vacant, Wolsey secured the post (September 1514). A year later he was elected a cardinal at Rome, and on Christmas Eve 1515 was sworn in as Lord Chancellor, the most important judicial office in England and a politically crucial position since it gave Wolsey the right to take the chair in the House of Lords and at meetings of the King's Council.

Wolsey saw the ceremony for the reception of his cardinal's hat from Rome as signalling the moment he had truly arrived. The hat was carried in a solemn procession by a papal prothonotary through the streets of London to Westminster Abbey, where it lay in state on the high altar for three days. Then, the ceremony began. Wolsey on his mule, with the nobles and all the southern bishops and their attendants, solemnly processed from his house at Westminster to the Abbey, where a special high mass was sung and a sermon preached. Wolsey was then consecrated a cardinal, his hat put upon his head in the manner of a royal coronation by the archbishop of Canterbury. *Te Deum* was sung, after which Wolsey returned home, the day ending with a magnificent feast attended by the royal family, all the nobles, and the judges.

Wolsey had proved his administrative genius by organizing Henry's earliest campaigns in France and Scotland, notably in 1513, when the king personally led his armies in an invasion of northern France, capturing Thérouanne and Tournai after the battle of the Spurs (16 August). These towns had little strategic value, but they delighted the king. Another invasion was planned, but when Henry's allies proved untrustworthy, Wolsey negotiated an Anglo-French entente (August 1514), marrying the king's younger sister Mary to King Louis XII of France. The peace crumbled when Louis died and Francis I succeeded him (1 January 1515). But Wolsey made fresh terms with France in 1518, transforming them into a dazzling European treaty. The pope, the Holy Roman Emperor, Spain, France, England, Scotland, Venice, Florence, and the Swiss forged, with others, a Treaty of Universal Peace with a provision for mutual aid in case of infractions.

At a stroke Wolsey made London the centre of Europe and Henry its arbiter. This *coup de théâtre* was all the more remarkable in that, originally, it had been the pope's plan, snatched away by

Wolsey. And in 1520, in the so-called 'Golden Valley' half-way between Guisnes and Ardres beside Calais, Wolsey stage-managed a glittering tournament and entertainment called 'the Field of Cloth of Gold' to accompany a peace conference in which Henry and Francis vied with each other on the jousting field and on the dance floor. When the peace collapsed, further campaigns in 1522 and 1523 would bring Henry's army to within 50 miles of Paris. After that, the best chance in all of Henry's reign for French conquests came when the king's ally and Katherine of Aragon's nephew, the Emperor Charles V, would defeat and capture King Francis at the battle of Pavia (24 February 1525). But when Charles deserted his ally, Wolsey and Henry made peace with France once more.

In the domestic sphere, Wolsey sought to make ambitious advances in the areas of justice, taxation, and economic policy. Claiming to be a reformer, he expanded the workloads and the jurisdictions of the courts of Chancery and Star Chamber over which he presided as Lord Chancellor, so as to offer 'equal and impartial justice' to rich and poor. He then attacked the illegal enclosure of arable land to make sheep runs—thought to be a principal cause of unemployment and rural depopulation (since far fewer workers were needed to look after the sheep)—bringing more than 250 greedy landlords into court. He fixed 'just prices' for meat and poultry in London and investigated the scarcity of victuals. And he hauled 74 provincial graziers into Star Chamber for operating a cartel, along with dozens of butchers.

In years of bad harvests, Wolsey's commissioners searched for hoarded grain supplies and ordered surplus stocks to be sent to market for immediate sale. In the sphere of social policy, he promoted education and supervised the building of the Savoy Hospital in London, which was modelled on the hospital of Santa Maria Nuova in Florence, where patients received professional medical care in separate wards for men and women as well as adequate nutrition. Finally, Wolsey devised what appears to have been a national population census in 1528 in connection with his survey of food supplies. If only more of its returns had survived, this might have been something for which he would have been celebrated by historical demographers.

To satisfy Henry's increasing demands for troops and money, Wolsey ordered a military survey in 1522 from which he learned that 128,250 able-bodied men were available for conscription (from 28 counties), that 35,000 coats of mail were in stock, and that a surprising one-third of the militia were archers. In parallel, he made strenuous efforts to increase the receipts of taxation and to shift the costs of payment away from the poor towards the rich. To deter underpayments, he insisted that taxpayers were individually assessed—if necessary on oath—by competent officials (supervised by himself), who had the power to examine and revise the assessments.

Wolsey raised substantial 'loans' from taxpayers in 1522 based on his new assessments, plus taxes between 1514 and 1527 that in total brought in £450,000 from the laity and £240,000 from the clergy (roughly £690 million in modern values). He raised hackles in 1523 by asking for far too much and had to reduce his demands, but he made his only serious error in 1525, when angry complaints in London and revolts in East Anglia taught him that it was impossible to levy new taxes without Parliament's consent.

Wolsey was to make himself so powerful that foreign ambassadors called him a 'second king' or *alter rex*. Less well known is that he also built networks in Italy, and especially at Rome, that enabled him to control and monitor—even often to monopolize—the channels of communications between England and the papacy. The diplomats who nicknamed him *alter rex* also called him a 'second pope' or *alter papa*. And when between them Henry and Wolsey bludgeoned the pope into granting Wolsey the rank of plenipotentiary papal legate, an appointment which he soon had extended for life, he became the highest ecclesiastical authority in the land.

In practice, despite convening a legatine council of bishops and senior clergy in 1519 and announcing the prospect of reform, Wolsey's church measures came to very little. He promulgated new 'constitutions' (or statutes) for the parochial clergy and a revised set for the Benedictine and Augustinian orders. Some further measures for monastic reform were considered, but did not lead to anything. Wolsey intervened in some 20 monastic elections, took part in eight or nine attempts to remove a monastic head (though on only four occasions were these efforts successful), and authorized 72 legatine visitations. He promoted a scheme to create 13 new English episcopal sees on monastic foundations in order to bring the dioceses into line with current population trends. He also advocated a plan to reduce the number of Irish archdioceses from four to two and dioceses from 30 to nine or ten, and to appoint only English candidates to them—but both schemes were left unfinished. Finally, with royal and papal approval, he redistributed the assets of some 30 monasteries to found colleges at Oxford and Ipswich, but failed to complete the legal transfer of resources to them before his fall, with disastrous consequences for the Ipswich college.

A call for spiritual renewal

With hindsight, Wolsey's papal legacy appears to have been a missed opportunity, ignoring a mounting release of forces among intellectuals and the literate at home and on the Continent aimed at spiritual renewal. Erasmus of Rotterdam had taken northern Europe by storm when he rejected medieval scholasticism in favour of the Gospels and a simple 'philosophy of Christ', embellishing his calls for a new spirit of evangelism with lacerating, scabrously witty critiques of priests and monks, and even the papacy itself. Erasmus was a close friend of Thomas More. He made four visits to England, and it was in Cambridge, on his last stay in 1511–14, that he began work on his new editions of the writings of St Jerome and of the Greek New Testament.

Thomas More's *Utopia* (1516) was more complex. Book I was a critique of existing society, while Book II wittily described an imaginary society living on a remote island supposedly visited by a mysterious sea-captain called 'Raphael Hythlodaeus' (the name means 'purveyor of nonsense') at the end of a voyage with the explorer Amerigo Vespucci to Brazil, when he failed to return to Europe with the rest of the crew. Living in accordance with principles of natural virtue, the Utopians possessed reason, but lacked Christian revelation, and by implicitly comparing their benign social customs and enlightened attitudes with the inferior standards, in practice, of Christian Europeans, More produced an indictment of the latter based largely on deafening silence. For the irony and scandal was that Christians had so much to learn from heathens.

But Erasmus's and More's world view was vulnerable. Henry had at first shown no visible sign of opposition to moderate church reform. But all this changed in 1520 when Pope Leo X condemned and excommunicated Martin Luther in the bull *Exsurge Domine*. And when shortly afterwards Henry had his attention drawn to Luther's book *The Babylonian Captivity of the Church* in which the rebel German monk claimed that only three of the seven Catholic sacraments had been instituted by Christ, the king felt he had no alternative but to take up his pen to defend doctrinal orthodoxy in a book entitled *Assertio Septem Sacramentorum* ('A Defence of the Seven Sacraments'), for which he earned himself the title of 'Defender of the Faith' from a grateful pope.

It should be said that the vast majority of Henry's subjects, especially those in the northernmost shires and borderlands, were still content with the traditional liturgies and beliefs of the Catholic Church. At parish level, religious confraternities (or societies of laity founded to honour the Virgin Mary or a saint) were flourishing even if candidates for the monastic life were fewer than before. Gifts to churches for building repairs, and especially to endow chantry chapels or colleges of priests to sing for the souls of the dead in purgatory, continued to be made on a significant scale.

But a vocal minority called for change. In London and the Thames Valley, the South-East and parts of East Anglia, areas with greater exposure to trading networks to the Continent, many people wanted a more meaningful, more personal spiritual experience than they felt the institutional Catholic Church could offer them. In particular, literate parishioners yearned to read the Bible, and chiefly the New Testament, in English rather than in the Latin Vulgate. However, vernacular Bibles had been illegal in England for over a century despite being permitted abroad, since the bishops believed that an English Bible, even an authorized one, would encourage heresy by permitting people to form their own religious opinions.

Luther, greatly assisted by the invention in Germany some 50 years before of printing with moveable metal type, eagerly promoted reading the 'Word of God' in the vernacular. In addition, he and his supporters taught that good works and the sacraments of the Catholic Church alone were insufficient for salvation. Instead, Luther preached a doctrine of 'justification by faith alone'. Grace, and therefore redemption, was solely at the will of a just, if merciful, God. True believers (or more strictly the 'elect'), he said, receive a gift of faith that has nothing to do with their own sinful actions on earth or those of the pope or the clergy.

When Luther's ideas and many books began to penetrate the universities, the London merchant guilds, and the lawyers' inns of court, the call for spiritual renewal became a potent force for change, expanding its agenda to include the reform of superstition and abuses. At Cambridge, those influenced included the preachers Robert Barnes and Thomas Bilney, who went out to spread the 'Word of God' in London and East Anglia. They attracted large audiences, who increasingly sought to found their faith on texts of Scripture. And at the inns of court, an organized network of secular lawyers who yearned to read an English Bible planned to check the jurisdiction of the church courts in cases of heresy and to make the clergy and church law accountable to the principles of a fair trial that they believed were offered by the verdicts of juries in the secular courts.

Although the Catholic Church had already begun to see the relevance of teaching the people the Creed, Lord's Prayer, and Ten Commandments in English instead of Latin, the pace of change was slow. This encouraged a Gloucestershire man educated at Wolsey's old college in Oxford, an ardent admirer of Erasmus's Greek New Testament, William Tyndale, to call on the bishop of London, Cuthbert Tunstall, offering to translate the New Testament. He was roundly rebuffed, but—refusing to accept defeat and privately sponsored by a sympathetic London merchant, Humphrey Monmouth—he left for Cologne, where he vowed to bring England over to Luther's side and began printing the first 22 chapters of St Matthew's Gospel. Forced to flee, he took refuge in the safe Lutheran city of Worms in late 1525, from where the following year he watched the first ever complete English New Testament roll off the presses.

Tyndale's New Testament was slow to take off, but was almost unstoppable once it did. The English Reformation had begun. Part of the tragedy, from the official Church's viewpoint, is that Tyndale lacked viable competition—to the frustration of Thomas More, who supported the idea of an authorized English Bible but deplored the Lutheran heresies that the bishops claimed had found their way into Tyndale's edition. The other part of the tragedy was Wolsey. By increasingly flaunting his power as a cardinal and papal legate, especially by the massive sums he spent on costly tapestries and building projects using church revenues, he provoked widespread criticism—by 1529, he was seen as a fundamental obstacle to change.

Wolsey saw these things from a completely different perspective. He believed that a Renaissance cardinal, especially one of low birth, had a duty to display his greatness and magnificence to the world as a prop to his authority. He held that it was fitting for a cardinal to use his wealth to honour his position within the Church, as long as he did not neglect social improvement, education, and the relief of the poor and sick, so that others might also benefit from his status.

In his *Practice of Prelates* (1530), Tyndale castigated Wolsey as a 'wily wolf' and the 'shipwreck of all England', a man 'so desirous and greedy of honour that he cared not but for the next and most compendious way thereto, whether godly or ungodly'. Tyndale's friends were blunter still:

> A great carl he is and fat,
> Wearing on his head a red hat,
> Procured with angels' subsidy…

By the time Henry's desire for an annulment of his marriage to Katherine of Aragon came to the fore, Wolsey had made enemies among the nobles and other members of the King's Council besides among his fellow churchmen and the London citizens, who howled with protest at his tax demands.

The problem of Henry's divorce

Although Katherine of Aragon had borne five children, all but one were stillborn or miscarried. The queen was blamed for her gynaecological misfortunes. However, it is possible that Henry could have been responsible, if he was positive for a blood group antigen, known as Kell, and Katherine—like 90 per cent of Caucasian populations—was negative. If this had been the case, a high proportion of the foetuses he fathered would have automatically died because his partner would make antibodies to attack the foetal red blood cells. Such a genetic mismatch—in

Katherine's case—is likely, because her sisters, Juana of Castile and Maria of Portugal, each produced living children with consummate ease, meaning they were probably Kell negative.

Of Henry and Katherine's children, Princess Mary (b. 1516) alone survived more than a few weeks. By 1527 at the latest, his first queen had passed the menopause and Henry still lacked a legitimate son, a matter of vital concern for a dynastic monarchy. With Elizabeth ('Bessie') Blount, one of his mistresses, he had a bastard son, Henry Fitzroy (b. 1519), whom he created Earl of Richmond and Somerset, but the boy was to die when he was just 17.

Henry's views on female succession would be set out in *c*.1531 in the preface to a pamphlet entitled *A Glasse of the Truthe*, the contents of which he personally vetted (and perhaps partly wrote). With his divorce from Katherine and the quest for a legitimate male heir then topping the agenda, the *Glasse* cautioned that if a woman 'shall chance to rule, she cannot continue long without a husband, which by God's law must then be her governor and head, and so finally shall direct the realm.'

Henry feared that a woman successor was a recipe for a fresh civil war, and when later in his reign he did finally concede that circumstances could arise in which a woman might succeed, he attempted to dictate precisely how she would be permitted to marry.

By 1527, Henry not only desired a male heir to settle the succession, he had fallen madly in love with Anne Boleyn, even sending his new secretary, William Knight, to Rome behind Wolsey's back to seek the necessary dispensations to marry her. It was a barefaced request, and yet royal matrimonial annulments were not uncommon, and all might have been resolved quickly had Henry not begun to insist on his divorce as a matter of principle. In essence, Henry came to believe that his marriage to Katherine was 'incestuous' and 'unnatural', and that the papal dispensation allowing him to marry his brother's widow in the first place had always been flawed, thereby taking the argument out of the realm of matrimonial law into that of hypersensitive papal power. For if the pope's dispensation was invalid, it must have been because a successor of St Peter had made a mistake or had no power to devise such instruments in the first place, making the pope no better than any other human legislator who had exceeded his authority.

In 1529, Wolsey at last obtained delegated powers from a reluctant Pope Clement VII to hear Henry's case, sitting jointly with Cardinal Campeggio at Blackfriars. Called to defend herself, Katherine made an emotional appeal for justice, throwing herself at Henry's feet, begging him to consider her helpless position as a foreigner, her obedience as a loyal and devoted wife, and her own and her daughter's honour. She then appealed to Rome as the only tribunal before which her case could properly be judged.

However, the court had to be adjourned before a final sentence could be given. At the last moment, Clement revoked the case to Rome, as he had always intended to do. From Henry's viewpoint it was a humiliating failure, only made worse when the pope wrote him a letter of apology, expressing his 'sorrow' at having been 'compelled' to revoke the case, and explaining that the diplomatic pressures on him both within and outside the Vatican were too great.

Henry had placed all his hopes on a successful outcome at the Blackfriars court, but now he was no further forward with his divorce suit and Katherine had appealed to Rome. Wolsey, it seemed, was increasingly a liability, since his power as a cardinal and plenipotentiary legate came from Rome. He simply had to go.

Chapter 3
The Reformation and British 'imperial' kingship

The break with Rome

In October 1529, Henry ousted Wolsey and appointed Thomas More as his new Lord Chancellor, but the move backfired since More was unable to support the divorce. Meanwhile, the king turned to new advisers. Steered by a coterie of stellar academics led by Edward Fox and Thomas Cranmer—both Cambridge scholars who were closely linked to the Boleyns—Henry started to investigate the 'true difference' between royal and ecclesiastical power. He began to look back to the golden days of the British 'imperial' past, to the time of the late-Roman Emperor Constantine and of King Lucius I, rulers to whom Henry believed God had given theocratic powers like King David and King Solomon in the Old Testament.

In fact, Lucius I had never existed: he was a myth, a figment of a medieval chronicler's fertile imagination. But Henry's British 'sources' showed that this Lucius had been a great ruler, the first Christian king of Britain, who had endowed the British Church with all its liberties and possessions and then written to Pope Eleutherius (who had existed), asking him to transmit the Roman laws. The pope's reply, however, explained that Lucius did not need any Roman law, because he already had the *lex Britanniae* which was a law sufficient unto itself:

> For you be God's vicar in your kingdom, as the psalmist says, 'Give
> the king thy judgments, O God, and thy righteousness to the king's
> son' (Ps. 72, 1)... A King hath his name of ruling, and not of having
> a realm. You shall be a king, while you rule well; but if you do
> otherwise, the name of a king shall not remain with you... God
> grant you so to rule the realm of Britain, that you may reign with
> him for ever, whose vicar you be in the realm.

Vicarius Dei—'vicar of Christ'. Henry's divorce had led him,
incredibly, to believe in his royal supremacy over the English
Church.

Until mid-1531 or thereabouts, Henry might still have been willing
to consider a trial of his divorce suit in a 'neutral' place other than
England or Rome if it could be arranged to his advantage. But
when More resigned in May 1532, Henry turned increasingly to
Thomas Cromwell, Wolsey's old fixer, who had thrown in his lot
with the Boleyns and served Henry as his parliamentary manager
for over a year. Cromwell, who was closely in touch with several of
the leading merchants in London and Antwerp, had very wide
experience of politics and statecraft, since he had lived in Florence
in his youth for a while when in the service of an Italian merchant,
and he had made three further brief visits to Italy in 1514 and
1517–18, travelling to Rome. He was not yet Wolsey's replacement
as chief minister, but was well on the way to grasping the levers of
power.

On 24 or 25 January 1533, Henry and a newly pregnant Anne
Boleyn were secretly (and bigamously) married at Greenwich
Palace. Spurred into action by her pregnancy, the king summoned
Parliament, which steadily threw off England's allegiance to
Rome, beginning in April 1533 with the Act in Restraint of
Appeals to Rome, drafted and pushed through by Cromwell.
When, in May, Cranmer, whom Henry made archbishop of
Canterbury, pronounced Henry and Katherine's divorce, Anne's
coronation festivities lasting a fortnight had already begun. And in

1534, Henry went on to declare himself the 'Supreme Head of the English Church'.

When honest dissenters like the leaders of the London Carthusians, Thomas More, and Bishop John Fisher refused to condone the king's second marriage or approve his new title of 'Supreme Head', Henry showed no mercy (Figure 3). To enforce his claims—and at Cromwell's suggestion—he revised and greatly extended the compass of the treason law to include a new crime of 'treason by words'. Anyone denying the king's new title or that Anne was the lawful queen, even by words alone, became vulnerable, and to ensure convictions, Cromwell drafted the indictments and rigged the juries at their trials. To flush out opposition, Henry and Cromwell set a test to ensure that no one would be likely to speak out against Henry's policy or his new queen. It took the form of oaths of allegiance, the first to be taken by all males over 14 and the second more selectively by the bishops and clergy, and by laymen holding public offices or those taking up their inheritances.

Anne's daughter, the future Queen Elizabeth, was born on 7 September 1533. Henry was bitterly disappointed that her baby was not the boy he expected even if, for the moment, he turned a brave face towards the world. But when Anne afterwards miscarried twice—in July 1534 and January 1536, the second time with a foetus said to be a 15-week-old boy—Henry took it into his head that God had damned his marriage to Anne, which must be unlawful.

Approaching his mid-40s, the king was fast becoming a dictatorial bully, wilful and blind to criticism. His mental state, perhaps exacerbated by the effects of a terrible jousting accident that had left him in a coma for two hours, was such that when in April 1536 Anne wilfully encouraged a preacher's criticism of the king's decision to seize the wealth of the smaller monasteries for the royal coffers rather than to found schools, universities, and hospitals, he decided that she had spoken out of turn once too often.

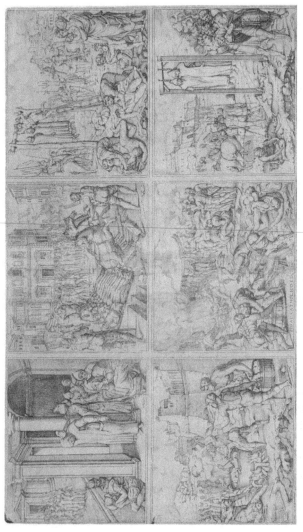

3. The hanging and disembowelling of the London Carthusians in 1535 for denying Henry VIII's new title of 'Supreme Head of the English Church'

Fickle in sexual matters for a decade or so, Henry had been dallying for some months with Jane Seymour, who had wisely chosen the motto 'Bound to obey and serve' and who, unlike Anne, quickly learned never to speak out of turn. Believing Jane would succeed where Anne had failed, the king lost no time in throwing his second wife to her court enemies. Once Henry made his decision on 1 May, Cromwell destroyed Anne and her supporters in a palace coup, accusing Anne of conspiring the king's death, an allegation he spiced up with further unproven charges of multiple adultery with some of the king's privy chamber intimates and incest with her brother, George. Anne and George were beheaded after treason trials at which it was expressly noted that no witnesses were called, enabling Henry to marry Jane without any of the trouble he had encountered with Katherine.

Thomas Cromwell

For the next four years, Henry governed through Cromwell, who finally secured the bulk of the power once exercised by Wolsey. The son of a Putney innkeeper, Cromwell had become an ally of the Boleyns after Wolsey's fall, only to turn on them in 1536. He had, as it appeared, his own agenda, promoting covertly a more radical religious policy than Henry was prepared to tolerate. Securing an appointment as Henry's (lay) Vicar-General and Vicegerent (or deputy) in Spiritual Affairs, he had the power to do everything that Wolsey had been able to do in church matters as well as attempting to settle the faith and doctrines of Henry's new Church of England.

Cromwell's administrative skills now surpassed even Wolsey's. As the king's Vicegerent, he masterminded an anti-papal campaign, which reached its zenith with the destruction of the shrine of England's only premier saint—Thomas Becket—at Canterbury in 1538 and the erasing of his (and the pope's) name from as many books and manuscripts as could be tracked down. In parallel, the new chief minister strove to reform and purge the Church on biblical lines, working with Cranmer and persuading a coterie of evangelical scholars and printers to assist him in disseminating tracts and translations with a decidedly reformist spin. True, Cromwell did not deny the Real Presence of Christ in the Eucharist nor teach Luther's doctrine of 'justification by faith alone' in so many words. As with the Lutheran Confession of Augsburg, Cromwell's Ten Articles (1536) and Injunctions to the Clergy (1536, 1538) simply 'lost' four of the Catholic sacraments, mentioning only the same three that Luther had said were valid because they had been instituted by Christ as the Gospels proved.

But his Injunctions attacked intercessions to saints and the use of images, seriously undermining belief in purgatory. They also unleashed the first iconoclasts, who (especially in London) set about destroying images of the pope and saints in statues and stained glass windows. On the more positive side, Cromwell took steps to improve the discipline and standards of the clergy especially where preaching was concerned. And in the sphere of social reform, he made new provisions for the education of children and poor relief, and decreed that young people should be put 'either to learning or to some other honest exercise, occupation or husbandry', lest they fall into idleness and begging.

Most notably, Cromwell was a patron of the complete English Bible produced in 1535 by Miles Coverdale and unofficially dedicated to the king—a risky enterprise since Henry, in the very same year, backed a new edition of the Latin Vulgate, for which he wrote the preface and chose the typeface. But Cromwell discovered that printing unabridged bibles in sufficient quantities for copies to be placed in all 8,500 parish churches was a massive challenge. To make it happen, he offered the printers £400 of his own money, plus other incentives, enabling them to publish a mass edition of a new 'Great Bible' in 1539, which Cromwell insisted be sold at a reduced price of 13s. 4d. per copy.

By then, Cromwell had almost completed the suppression of the monasteries. Two years after Henry had closed the smaller ones and seized their property, Cromwell began the attack on the greater houses. Deeply resented, the work of suppression was severely disrupted during the autumn and winter of 1536–7 by large-scale (and partly linked) revolts mainly in Lincolnshire and Yorkshire, mass protests involving as many as 60,000 people that were ruthlessly crushed by exemplary public hangings and a wholesale breach of Henry's promises to the rebel leaders. These risings gained support from a wide range of different social groupings, not just the poor, and from people with a disparate variety of complaints, since many northerners also had economic grievances against their landlords. The rebels came perilously close to success—a royal army of 30,000 men was needed to bring the disorders to a close.

Once stability had been restored, the monastic plunder was swiftly completed. Some 560 monastic institutions had been suppressed by November 1539, by which time lands valued at £132,000 per annum (£132 million in modern values) along with jewels, precious metal, and other valuables worth £75,000 had been confiscated.

The effects of the suppression may conveniently be split into those which were planned, and those not. Within the former category, Henry and Cromwell eliminated the last centres of organized resistance to the royal supremacy. Above all, the king's regular income was almost doubled. But for how long? The irony would be that Henry's debts, combined with his profligacy as a builder of palaces and as a warmonger, would so erode the gains from the suppression as to cancel out the longer-term benefits. The king would soon be forced to sell large tranches of ex-monastic lands to meet his current fiscal needs, not to mention his need to appease the laity's demand for a share of the booty.

Of the unplanned effects, the wholesale destruction of fine abbey and priory buildings, melting down of medieval metalwork and jewellery, and sacking of libraries changed the cultural and sometimes the physical landscape. The clergy suffered an immediate decline in morale. The number of candidates for ordination dropped sharply—there was little real conviction that Henry's Reformation had anything to do with spiritual life, or with God. The disappearance of the abbots from the House of Lords meant that the ecclesiastical vote withered away, leaving the laity dominant in both Houses. And since the monasteries had possessed the right to appoint two-fifths of the parochial clergy, these rights were transferred to the laity when the ex-religious lands were sold, enabling the gentry to veto or approve their parish clergy.

Of the wider socio-economic consequences, the chief were the rise of a newly buoyant land market and a massive release of wealth in favour of courtiers and the gentry. The worst social effects were felt in northern England and Wales, where the abbeys had provided a higher proportion of employment and poor relief than they had elsewhere.

Cromwell's ascendancy came to an abrupt end in June 1540, when his Court enemies accused him of advancing the religious Reformation too zealously. By then, Henry had stepped back from moves to redefine church doctrine by asking Parliament to pass an Act of Six Articles (1539) that reversed much of the thrust of Cromwell's policy as Vicegerent and affirmed all seven of the Catholic sacraments at least in name, even if the king could sometimes be personally ambiguous on the theology of the mass and had a number of decidedly maverick ideas on the priesthood and auricular confession.

When the Duke of Norfolk showed Henry irrefutable evidence that his second chief minister had secretly protected a group of radical Protestants at Calais, Cromwell was arrested and 'attainted' (i.e., convicted by Parliament) on charges of heresy and treason, and beheaded. When at last the scales fell from the king's eyes, he came to see his former confidant as little more than a closet Lutheran.

Cromwell had inadvertently written his own epitaph in 1538 when he said in reply to taunts, 'My prayer is, that God give me no longer life, than I shall be glad to use mine office in edification, and not in destruction.' 'Edification' was an evangelical buzzword, meaning a deep spiritual understanding among true believers who had accepted the reformers' Gospel and sought to build the kingdom of God in this world. And Cromwell went further, saying of his duty to God, 'I do not cease to give thanks that it hath pleased His goodness to use me as an instrument and to work somewhat by me, so I trust I am ready to serve Him in my calling to my little power.' Often said by his admirers to be the first purely secular politician and a precursor of the modern age, Cromwell was in fact driven as much by his religious convictions as was Thomas More on the opposite side.

British 'imperial' kingship

His sights set ever higher once he believed himself to be rightfully the 'Supreme Head of the English Church', Henry in and after 1534 embarked on a series of projects seeking to outclass the achievements of his father. Eager to resume the more interventionist and centralizing policies that Henry VII had begun, Henry found that his new ideas of kingship tempted him into asserting a wider territorial 'empire' within the British Isles. Admittedly the northern shires, along with Wales and Ireland, were part of his dominions already, but more in name than in fact as the revolts of 1536–7 would convincingly prove. In any case, Henry wanted to go much further, actively seeking to conquer or subordinate Scotland and turn it into a satellite state of England.

Scotland was, of course, an independent kingdom ruled by James V, except that he happened to be Henry's nephew, since his mother, Margaret, who had married James IV in 1503, was the English king's elder sister. This encouraged Henry to reassert Scotland's dynastic dependency, reawakening dreams of Anglo-Scottish union. Earlier in his reign, Henry had revived King Edward I's claim to be 'superior' and 'overlord' of Scotland, a line he took most audibly in 1523 when considering crossing the frontier with a battle army. But his slogans subtly changed after the break with Rome, when he began to maintain that Wales, Ireland, and (increasingly) Scotland were 'within the orb of the "imperial crown" of England'.

On the eve of the Act of Supremacy in 1534, Henry feared that a group of regional nobles was plotting to overthrow him. The frontier with Scotland had long been a running sore. Still vaguely defined on a map, it was poorly policed and thieves crossed to and fro. Local, largely independent nobles and gentry—most of them staunchly Catholic and pro-papal—kept the peace, but holding their posts almost on a hereditary basis, they were regarded by their rivals and subordinates as criminals. While such criticism was often unfair, Henry was listening to their enemies and questioned especially the loyalty of Lord Dacre of Gilsland, whom he suspected of treason.

Ireland also posed an ongoing threat, since outside the Pale (the area around Dublin where English rule was concentrated), the Gaelic lords were loyal Catholics who refused to pay taxes or abandon Brehon law or customs. After the pretender Lambert Simnel had been crowned in Dublin, Henry VII had secured their loyalty by delegating royal power to a trusted magnate family: the Fitzgeralds, Earls of Kildare. By combining a sufficient following in the Pale with their power in the Gaelic community, the Fitzgeralds had performed a juggling act that had kept Ireland stable for almost 30 years.

Wales was less remote and the gentry more malleable, but still dangerous. English law had for years been disregarded in the Principality and marcher lordships, where conflicts of jurisdiction enabled suspects to flee from one lordship to another. Jurors could easily be corrupted and guns had been fired in the law-courts. After the break with Rome, Henry came to regard Wales chiefly as a haven for 'popish' insurgents. He was the more concerned because Welsh levies and horses formed the backbone of the royal army, and the favoured route for transporting troops to Ireland was through the (then) port of Chester.

In 1534, Cromwell sent a powerful group of royal councillors into Wales with orders to root out 'papists' and equipped with an official dispensation to try treasons and felonies summarily using English law. Such efforts culminated in Acts of Union (1536 and 1543) assimilating the medieval Principality and marcher lordships into 12 shires subject to English law, complete with parliamentary representation at Westminster and a court system modelled on the English assizes. English county administration was extended to Wales and a refurbished Council of Wales established at Ludlow Castle.

Henry, meanwhile, pounced on Lord Dacre and the Fitzgeralds. In 1534, Dacre was put on trial for treason and astonishingly found not guilty—he was the only nobleman to be acquitted in a treason trial during the reign. This did not deter Henry, who simply rearrested his victim before exacting an astronomical fine of £10,000 and forbidding Dacre to travel more than ten miles from London.

By then, Henry had taken the ninth Earl of Kildare into custody in England and sent him to the Tower, intending to charge him with treason, but was shocked to discover that the arrest sparked a spectacular revolt in Ireland. Thomas Fitzgerald, Lord Offaly ('Silken Thomas'), the Earl's heir, denounced Henry as a heretic and ordered anyone born in England to leave Ireland on pain of death. He threatened to ally with the pope and Charles V, and boasted that 12,000 Catholic troops were on their way to Ireland. Soon the country had been convulsed: Dublin Castle was besieged and the rebels went on an orgy of looting and burning, firing artillery in the streets and terrifying the citizens.

It took a vast English army until August 1535 to suppress the Irish revolt, costing 1,500 soldiers' lives and £40,000. Henry hanged or beheaded the ringleaders, but his methods turned the struggle into something approaching a Gaelic war of independence, committing him to a costly and lengthy policy of 'anglicizing' Ireland. This explains why, in 1541, he altered his official style from 'Lord' to 'King' of Ireland. He was incensed by Irish taunts that his 'regal estate' there was granted by the pope, referring to Adrian IV's bull *Laudabiliter*, which in 1155 had granted lordship over Ireland to the Anglo-Normans and implied that the king of England held Ireland as a papal vassal.

In Scotland, Henry continued to try and intimidate James V, repeatedly seeking to prevent him from allying with France or Spain, if that involved Scotland continuing to support the pope. Several of Henry's Catholic critics had already escaped from his clutches across the border—as had James Griffyd ap Powell, a silver-tongued Welsh rebel, who had talked his way out of the Tower, escaping with his wife and children to Scotland, where he asked for James's backing for a Welsh revolt against Henry.

Henry at last lost patience with James for allowing Scots to join the Irish revolt. He knew he was unable to fight on several fronts at once, so at first he tried conciliation, admitting his nephew to the Order of the Garter and sending him a remarkable letter justifying his theory of kingship and royal supremacy. When James ignored it, Henry threatened war, provoking James into his own 'imperial' claims and marriage to a French princess in 1537 to cement the 'auld alliance' between France and Scotland. Although his bride tragically died, James quickly chose another, the sensationally beautiful Mary of Guise. Thereafter, Henry's determination to conquer Scotland as well as lands in France became a burning obsession until his death.

Henry's later years

After suppressing the worst of the revolt in Ireland, Henry could at last focus again on the succession. In 1537, after an uneventful pregnancy, Jane Seymour had given birth to Prince Edward—finally Henry had a legitimate male heir. Although Jane succumbed to an infection and died shortly afterwards, she had done what was expected of her (Figure 4).

In January 1540, on Cromwell's advice, the king married Anne of Cleves to win European allies against the pope and the emperor. However, Anne, placid but plain, did not suit—and divorce was easy as the union had never been consummated. The marriage became another nail in Cromwell's coffin, after which Henry chose Katherine Howard, a girl barely out of her teens. But after what appears to have been 18 months of infatuation for Henry, she was caught in adultery with an old flame, causing the king to burst into tears and complain of his 'ill luck in meeting with such ill-conditioned wives'.

4. Henry VIII acquired the manor of Oatlands in Surrey in 1537 while Jane Seymour was pregnant. He promptly began building a new summer palace for them, which included a magnificent polygonal lantern tower from which the countryside could be viewed, but Jane was dead long before it was completed

After beheading the queen and her lover, Henry took Katherine Parr as his sixth and final queen. Already twice widowed, she was intelligent, cultivated, and pious, a model stepmother and ready—or so she was careful to pretend—to be guided in all things by her husband, and especially in religion. Her true religious sympathies, which were towards the evangelical reformers, she deftly disguised. Little more than 30 on the day she married Henry, she was vivacious and pretty with auburn hair, grey eyes, and a passion for fine clothes and smart shoes. Had she not been sexually attractive, she would never have caught Henry's attention. And it is unlikely that he would have married her if he had not believed her fecund, as he yearned for more sons.

Henry's plans for war in his final years would resurrect all his youthful dreams of conquest. By 1541, he had rebuilt his bridges with Charles V, paving the way for fresh campaigns against France, but was prudent enough to hesitate. James V had agreed to meet him at York to discuss settling their differences, but he committed the supreme offence of failing to turn up. In October 1542, therefore, an army under the Duke of Norfolk's command invaded Scotland, at first achieving little. It was the Scottish counter-stroke that destroyed all James's hopes. On 24 November, 3,000 English soldiers defeated 10,000 Scots at the battle of Solway Moss: the news of the disgrace killed James within a month. Scotland was left hostage to the fortunes of his daughter, the baby Mary, Queen of Scots, born only six days before her father died.

Despite this, Henry turned advantage into danger, over-extending himself with a strategy that sought to balance a succession of increasingly arrogant political and military interventions in Scotland with war against France. It was a policy that also partially wrecked the English economy, since, to pay for the war, Henry from 1542 onwards was forced to debase the coinage repeatedly as well as sell off the lion's share of the ex-monastic lands.

In 1543, Henry used the prisoners taken at Solway Moss as the nucleus of an anglophile party in Scotland, forcing on the Scots the Treaty of Greenwich, which projected an Anglo-Scottish dynastic union in the shape of a future marriage between Prince Edward and Mary, Queen of Scots. When, however, this anglophile party collapsed and the Scottish Parliament repudiated the treaty, Henry sent the Earl of Hertford—Jane Seymour's brother and Henry's finest commander—north with 12,000 men. Henry wanted to be revenged on the Scots for their disavowal of the treaty, warning the citizens of Edinburgh that he would 'exterminate' them 'to the third and fourth generations' if they stood in his way.

Hertford's devastation of the border country and the Lowlands in May 1544 was brutally effective, but culpably counter-productive. By sacking and burning Edinburgh, he united the Scots against what they viscerally depicted as English terrorism.

Henry, meanwhile, was cultivating Charles V as an ally. Reverting to tactics similar to those used by Wolsey in 1522 and 1523, he was planning a combined invasion of France that was to begin in June 1544 as soon as Hertford's crack troops had finished in Scotland and could be shipped across to Calais. The emperor was to march into France through Champagne, the English king through Picardy, and their armies were to converge on Paris. Each was to consist of 35,000 soldiers and 7,000 cavalry.

But Charles was seduced by peace proposals from King Francis. His invasion was half-hearted and the combined attack, predictably, was not concerted. Deluding himself into overconfidence by quickly capturing the town and port of Boulogne, Henry sought to dictate the entire course of the war, causing Charles to agree a separate peace with France at Crépi and leaving England's flank exposed.

The bulk of Henry's forces remained in France until June 1546, when Francis agreed that England could keep Boulogne for eight years, provided it was then returned complete with Henry's expensive new fortifications. When the agreement was ratified, Francis, in return, suspended his aid to the Scots, endorsing by implication the terms of the Treaty of Greenwich.

But as far as Scotland was concerned, Henry's 'Rough Wooing' (as it came to be known) of the young Scottish queen had backfired badly. Within two years, Mary would be shipped to France and pledged to marry the Dauphin when she was old enough, triggering a slow-burning fuse that would explode catastrophically 20 years later.

The death of Henry VIII

In his early 50s, Henry was seen to deteriorate physically. Corpulent and sometimes walking with a staff, his chest expanded to 58 inches and his waist to 54. He was in near-constant pain from an ulcerated left leg (eventually both legs were affected), possibly the result of varicose veins, more likely of osteomyelitis caused by bone splinters resulting from his hunting or jousting accidents. In his last few years the great royal beds at Whitehall and Hampton Court had to be extended to take the huge mass of the king's body and he was pushed about, to and fro, around his galleries and chambers in two special chairs called 'trams' (i.e., wheelchairs). At Oatlands Palace in Surrey, a special ramp was constructed to allow him to mount his hunters.

By the time he was 55, having ruled for almost 38 years, his physical decline was swift. Contrary to a common myth, he never suffered from syphilis. His apothecary's bills survive, showing that the drugs administered to him did not include mercury, which would certainly have been used if venereal disease was suspected. Rather it was gluttony, bad diet, and lack of exercise since his jousting accident that had transformed Henry from a companionable, ebullient, statuesque athlete into an immobile, vindictive autocrat, forever suspecting plots and factions, as much from his friends as his enemies.

Henry died in the early hours of Friday, 28 January 1547. He had successfully defied the pope, enlarged the power of the monarchy, and established the Church of England, giving it the broad shape it would retain for 400 years. With Wolsey's and Cromwell's aid, his dynasty had discovered how to make a lasting impression at home and abroad. Religious wars had been prevented and revolts suppressed. The clergy had been subordinated to the monarchy, Parliament's power had been increased and a wider territorial 'empire' asserted within the British Isles as a whole.

Against this, Henry's subversion of the law when it suited him and his utter ruthlessness with loyal servants and enemies alike verged on tyranny, while his idea of the Reformation was like a beached whale: stranded mid-way between the competing values of Catholicism and Protestantism. Besides breaking with the pope, he had denied as he grew older that the traditional orders of priesthood were ordained by God and whenever he encountered the words 'Holy Orders', he impatiently struck out the adjective, but he continued to reject the Lutheran doctrine of 'justification by faith alone'.

Possessed of a ruthless streak from his earliest days, Henry always looked for scapegoats when things went wrong and his vision of himself as 'Supreme Head of the English Church' could turn into a murderous paranoia. For his invasive demands of allegiance, he would be compared to the Sultan of Turkey and to the Roman emperors Nero and Tiberius. A supreme egoist, he was, despite all this, one of the strongest and most remarkable rulers to sit on the English throne.

Chapter 4
Mid-Tudor crisis
and the succession

Henry VIII's succession settlement

When Henry died he left a will in which, fearing a power struggle when his 9-year-old son succeeded him, he attempted to continue to rule from beyond the grave. Before leaving with his armies for France in 1544, he had got Parliament to pass an Act of Succession—his third attempt at legislation to settle this problem—that laid down the order of succession and gave legal force to his will. The Act declared that the succession would fall, in turn, to his son Edward and his lawful heirs, then to his daughter Mary and her lawful heirs, and finally to Elizabeth, with the proviso that Henry—who was as confident as ever that female rule was a dangerous risk—might devise specific rules for the succession of both his daughters by letters patent or in his will.

The 1544 Act made the inheritance of Mary and Elizabeth strictly conditional. Each would be excluded from the succession if she married without the 'assent and consent' of those privy councillors whom Henry named in his will or as many of them as were still living. If either of his daughters disobeyed, she would lose her place. And if both were disqualified, then by the king's will the throne would pass, in turn, to the heirs of Henry's nieces, the Ladies Frances and Eleanor Brandon, the daughters of his younger sister Mary, who had married Charles Brandon, Duke of

Suffolk, as her second husband. Should this so-called 'Suffolk line' fail, then the throne was to go to the 'next rightful heirs'.

That final clause is ambiguous, but it is important to notice that in his will Henry had not specifically *excluded* Mary, Queen of Scots, granddaughter of his elder sister Margaret, from the succession, as is commonly believed, even if he failed to mention her in her rightful hereditary place. Legally, the young Scottish queen was still entitled to inherit the throne as a residuary legatee (i.e., as 'the next rightful heir') by the king's will if all else failed.

Minority and female rule were topics that provoked irrational fears and stereotyped impulses in a deeply patriarchal society. The rule of a male minor was much easier to accept than that of a woman. The precedents were relatively clear: government would be exercised by a council of regency until the young king was declared 'of age'. In addition, a Protector of the Realm and a Governor of the King's Person might be appointed (these positions held either by a single person or split between two) to pronounce the boy-king's will in consultation with the regency council and to oversee his education and bringing-up.

By his will, Henry appointed 16 privy councillors to govern in his son's name until he was 18 (Figure 5). Twelve other individuals were to assist and be 'of counsel' to them. The council's members were to govern by majority decision and there was no provision made in the will for the appointment of a single regent.

On 31 January 1547, Henry's will was read to the regency council. But within six weeks, Hertford—who created himself Duke of Somerset—was able to break it after inveigling a majority of Edward's councillors into making him Lord Protector and Governor of the King's Person. Now a fresh grant of letters patent gave Somerset near-sovereign powers as regent until Edward was 18.

5. Edward VI holding a leather purse in one hand and a red rose in the other. To the left among the roses and violets is a sunflower (the colour now faded), that instead of turning to the sun as heliotropic plants do, turns to the young king, who is eulogized in Italian and Latin texts below

As Protector, Somerset took what (legally) were tantamount to monarchical powers, enabling him to appoint anyone he chose to the Privy Council. To stimulate consent, he further ennobled and rewarded the members of the regency council with generous grants of land. Almost certainly, he had their broad support at first, even if his younger brother, Thomas Seymour, was desperately jealous and coveted the post of Governor of the King's Person for himself.

But the regency councillors almost certainly imagined that Somerset was merely to be their executive agent, not quasi-king. They envisaged that as Protector, Somerset would continue to consult them about key policy decisions and not attempt to rule by himself in Edward's name. The tension dramatically increased when Somerset made critical decisions about entering into wars with Scotland and France, about domestic security and the economy in England and Ireland, and about the advance of the Protestant Reformation in ways that his fellow councillors considered to be arbitrary and ill-informed.

Somerset played political poker for the highest possible stakes. He snubbed the nobility and gentry, appealing over their heads to the mass of lesser yeomen, craftsmen, artisans, and commoners outside the elite, purporting to understand their problems and be on their side. In short, he courted popularity. It was a ploy that Robert Devereux, Earl of Essex, would also adopt in the later years of Elizabeth's reign, but on a narrower front and from a more solid base of support than that enjoyed by Somerset.

The threat of a mid-Tudor crisis

Somerset from the outset decided to reinforce Henry VIII's largely successful anti-papal campaign with a further reformation of church doctrine. Archbishop Cranmer provided much of the spiritual leadership, but Somerset controlled the pace at which the reform programme proceeded. In 1547, the Protector lifted the restrictions the old king had imposed on the printing press and reissued Thomas Cromwell's Injunctions to the Clergy. And in 1548, by an order of the Privy Council, the iconoclasts were encouraged to smash stained-glass windows, paint over Catholic religious art with whitewash, and destroy images and cults of saints.

Somerset next persuaded Parliament to suppress chantries, colleges of priests and religious confraternities, and transfer their assets to the king. A further land confiscation followed, which the Protector justified as abolishing the 'superstition' of the doctrine of purgatory and prayers for the dead, but which the Privy Council privately admitted was to relieve the king's 'charges and expenses, which do daily grow and increase'.

Not content with this, Somerset ordered inventories to be made of the wealth of all 8,500 parish churches initially on a diocesan basis, stiffening up his inquisition early in 1549, when carefully selected lay commissioners were appointed to do the task systematically county by county.

Although Henry VIII had retained the Latin mass and most other church services almost exactly as they had been said before the break with Rome, he had allowed the Litany to be said in English. Somerset now went considerably further, letting Cranmer devise a new liturgy in English for the service of Holy Communion in 1548 as an experiment, and the following year authorizing a comprehensive reform of church liturgies in the First Book of Common Prayer. Prepared by a committee of theologians steered by Cranmer, the new Prayer Book was debated and approved by Parliament and enforced by an Act of Uniformity. Unfortunately, the reforms lacked an officially defined theology of the Eucharist and proved extraordinarily divisive.

A cacophony of competing Protestant voices complained that the reforms were botched, while traditional Catholics seethed with resentment and saw an opportunity to take their revenge. The single achievement of the reforms from an evangelical perspective was to allow communion in both the bread and the wine. Somerset claimed that his approach was bipartisan, but in reality he was caught in a trap of his own making, seeking to appease Charles V, whose neutrality towards England he wished to guarantee at a time when the country was at war with Scotland and France, while at the same time appealing for the support of a growing number of articulate Protestants.

Meanwhile, a series of economic and social issues became critical, made worse by religious grievances. Of the economic factors, the chief was demographic change. In 1525, the population was only around 2.26 million. By 1547, it topped 3 million. The consequential rise in demand and pressure on available resources of food and clothing within a society that was still overwhelmingly agrarian were severely compounded by inflation, in some considerable part caused by Henry's currency debasements since 1542, which had increased the quantity of money circulating in the economy by more than a third.

Soaring demand for land and food encouraged land speculators. Land hunger led to soaring rents. Tenants of farms and copyholders (i.e., those holding their lands by manorial custom rather than as leasehold estates) were evicted by commercially astute landlords. Several adjacent farms would be conjoined and amalgamated for profit by outside investors, at the expense of sitting tenants. Marginal (and sometimes arable) land was enclosed and converted to pasture for more profitable sheep-rearing (Figure 6). Commons were enclosed and waste land reclaimed, with consequent extinction of common grazing rights. If that were not enough, a vigorous market arose among dealers in defective titles to land, with resulting harassment of many legitimate occupiers.

High agricultural prices also encouraged market racketeers or gave farmers strong incentives to produce crops for sale in the dearest markets in nearby towns. Between *c.*1525 and 1550, cereal prices rose almost threefold and wool prices doubled, as did the prices of meat, poultry, and vegetables. In the same period the average wage of an agricultural labourer dropped by a quarter in real terms and that of a building craftsman dropped by around a third. Matters were made worse when Somerset began debasing the coinage again in 1548, triggering an artificial export boom for unfinished woollen cloth that within three years would be followed by a severe trade depression.

As the mix of religious changes fused with the wider socio-economic crisis, the leaders of the Privy Council urged Somerset to

6. The double-wheeled plough was drawn by horses or oxen double abreast, and was indispensable for arable farmers working on flinty or gravelly soil struggling to plough more than one acre a day. Enclosure of marginal arable land for more profitable sheep farming posed a threat to the labourers who operated the ploughs and put many of them out of work

take strong measures quickly to prevent mass discontent leading to disorder and revolt. The Protector's response was to issue letters and proclamations attacking enclosures and appointing commissioners to reform them. In doing so, he not only exceeded his legal powers but appeared to be dangerously appeasing the masses by professing to be on their side. By attempting to fix prices nationally for basic foodstuffs (but at terrifyingly high metropolitan levels) and supporting in Parliament a new tax on sheep and woollen cloth, he actually increased discontent rather than quelling it. To the nobles and gentry, it seemed deeply threatening, almost as if Somerset was seeking a political partnership between government and commoners that might reduce the privileges of the elite.

Somerset's wars

Somerset's most spectacular failure was his foreign policy. Deeply committed ideologically to Henry's policy towards Scotland in the 1540s and to the defunct Treaty of Greenwich, his obsession was to revive and bring to fruition Henry's plan to subdue French influence in Scotland and achieve the union of the crowns by a marriage between Edward and Mary, Queen of Scots.

Invading Scotland in September 1547, he first won the battle of Pinkie and then built and garrisoned forts largely concentrated on the border with England and the East coast. Incurring astronomical costs in excess of £500,000 (£500 million in modern values) and hiring mercenaries from Germany and Italy to boost his forces, the Duke justified his efforts as an attempt to unite the British Isles and free Scotland from Franco-papal tyranny, but the cause of the Scottish religious reformers was hardly helped by a policy that pushed Scotland ever closer into the embrace of Catholic France.

In June 1548, 6,000 French troops landed at Leith and the young Mary, Queen of Scots, was removed to France. When Somerset

Mid-Tudor crisis and the succession

continued to threaten Scotland, King Henry II of France declared war on England. Faced with impossible odds, Somerset offered to return Boulogne immediately rather than waiting until 1554 as previously agreed, but negotiations collapsed when the French king demanded Calais as well. So Somerset had to send fresh troops to France and strengthen the fortifications at Calais and Boulogne, moves that required a new round of coinage debasements and heavy taxation, supplemented by borrowing and further sales of ex-monastic and other church lands.

As if in chorus, radical Protestant preachers—seeing the rapidly declining standard of living enjoyed by the commoners as prices soared—began attacking greed, 'covetousness', and 'commodity' (i.e., the rush for profits) as the root of the social problem. Some, such as Robert Crowley and Hugh Latimer, began preaching a Gospel of liberty and the kingdom of God in this world. Even as economic conditions fuelled by religious fears turned into a crisis, and 'stirs' and protests began to take shape over much of southern England, Somerset issued a fresh series of letters and protestations in which he again appeared to side with the poor and appealed to the masses for their support against his critics in the Privy Council.

The 'commotion time' of 1549 and the fall of Protector Somerset

In May 1549 'stirs' and popular protests led by commoners erupted in Somerset, Wiltshire, Hampshire, Kent, Sussex, and Essex as people claimed that a conspiracy of landowners had obstructed Somerset's enforcement of legislation against enclosures. Devon and Cornwall rose in June, followed by Norfolk and Suffolk and eight other counties including Oxfordshire in July, with further risings in August. Of these, the largest were in East Anglia and the western counties. No single cause was responsible, but socio-economic grievances topped the list in East Anglia, while religious changes—partly the new Book of Common

Prayer and partly grievances over the Protector's suppression of the chantries and colleges—were predominant in Oxfordshire and in the Western Rising.

The East Anglian rising was led by Robert Kett, a successful butcher and tanner from Wymondham in Norfolk who also had extensive landholdings and was a man of considerable leadership talents. The rising gained its support initially at the celebrations for the feast of St Thomas Becket at Wymondham from which Kett's section of the revolt stemmed—this even though Henry VIII and Cromwell had declared Becket to be 'a rebel and a traitor to his prince' and abolished his feast day. Further large support for the rising came from those attending major markets and fairs held at Sudbury and Stowmarket in Suffolk.

Beginning with an attack on those responsible for enclosures, the rising swelled to a gathering of between 16,000 and 20,000 men, who camped outdoors on Mousehold Heath outside Norwich from 10 July until their final defeat by a royal army on 27 August. Kett, it is alleged, issued warrants for the muster of supplies of food and weapons, and for the destruction of enclosures and the imprisonment of local gentry. The protesters also established a representative council which drew up a list of grievances. Most famously, Kett is said to have dispensed justice both to his own followers and unpopular local gentry beneath a tree known as the 'oak of reformation'.

In the West Country, the 1549 rising was preceded the previous year by the assassination in Helston in West Cornwall of William Body, a reforming archdeacon. Whether the murder was a dress rehearsal for the events of 1549 is hotly disputed, but since the assassins boldly declared that anyone who embraced 'new fashions' in religion would perish in the same way, it is likely that it was. Within a few days 3,000 West Cornishmen were up in arms; order was restored by the gentry only with outside help.

Then, in 1549, the main rising began at Bodmin, in mid-Cornwall. The Cornishmen, whose strong sense of regional identity had not dimmed since their revolt of 1497 against Henry VII's taxation, seem to have believed that by imposing Protestantism on them, Somerset would force Englishness on them too.

Both the Devon and Cornish commoners attacked the Protector's new Prayer Book, claiming that they disliked the liturgy in English and preferred Latin. Spreading rapidly throughout Devon and Cornwall, the rising was the more dangerous since the protesters exploited factional divisions among the gentry. Socio-economic grievances were also aired as the Devon men condemned Somerset's tax on sheep and woollen cloth and appealed for relief against high food prices.

The rising in Cornwall, meanwhile, was reinforced by the support of disenchanted lesser gentry such as Humphrey Arundell of Helland, a man passed over by the Crown as a local magistrate. Like Kett, a capable administrator, Arundell played a crucial role in mobilizing the commoners. But events spun swiftly out of control when Arundell and his allies found that the leaders of the mob had turned against the established gentry—'Kill the gentlemen and we will have the Six Articles up again and ceremonies as they were in King Henry VIII's time', they were alleged to have proclaimed. The protesters saw the gentry as the chief enforcers of Somerset's religious changes and believed that only when they were rid of them could the old religion fully be restored.

Somerset dithered over the revolts in the spring of 1549, not wishing to disrupt his Scottish campaign. He relied for too long on a mixture of pardons and proclamations—a policy of leniency—and was severely criticized by his fellow privy councillors for ignoring their advice. In July the Protector at last ordered military reprisals without scruple and cancelled his Scottish project. The revolts were brutally suppressed using Genoese and German mercenaries: 2,500 westerners were slain and Kett lost 3,000 men.

But the defeat of the rebels came too late for Somerset. A putsch (i.e., a violent attempt to overthrow the government) against him quickly followed, led by his chief rival in the Privy Council, John Dudley, Earl of Warwick—the eldest son of the executed Edmund Dudley and a pragmatic realist who had first risen to power and influence as a naval commander in Henry VIII's last wars. His strike was preceded by an attack on Somerset's unstable brother, Thomas Seymour. Charged with attempting to seize Edward and take him 'into [his] own hands and custody' and also with attempting to marry the king's half-sister Elizabeth, Seymour was attainted in Parliament for treason, and beheaded.

The attack on Somerset himself followed in October 1549. Articles of impeachment accused the Protector of governing ineffectively and of failing to consult his colleagues, or else of summoning them only occasionally and 'for the name's sake' to approve decisions he had taken already. It did not suit Warwick to have Somerset tried and beheaded for another two years, but within hours of his putsch he and his closest allies had taken lodgings close to Edward's 'to give good order for the government of his most royal person'.

The rule of John Dudley, Duke of Northumberland

Warwick's realignment of the Privy Council was complete by February 1550. Shunning the title of Lord Protector, he instead took that of Lord President of the Council, seeking to dampen fears that he wanted quasi-regal powers. Creating himself Duke of Northumberland in October 1551, he made a determined effort to reverse the mess left by Somerset. Once domestic peace was restored, he set about putting the country's finances back on course through a programme of sustained reforms and retrenchments in spending, including a revaluation of the coinage.

Although this last was ineptly done—the deflationary change was bungled by announcing it on 30 April 1551 but fixing the date at which it was to become effective at 31 August, thereby allowing an interlude of four months in which speculators could thrive—it gave some immediate, if temporary relief to consumers and set the Crown's fiscal policy on the road to long-term recovery.

Above all, Northumberland swiftly ended Somerset's disastrous wars with Scotland and France. To this end, he had a simple expedient—he sought peace with dishonour, a humiliating but highly attractive alternative to fighting. Boulogne was surrendered to France at once in return for 400,000 crowns. Somerset's garrisons in Scotland were abandoned and their forces discharged, and the Treaty of Greenwich was quietly forgotten. It thus became inevitable that Mary, Queen of Scots, would marry the Dauphin, but such were their ages that the wedding could not take place until April 1558.

Northumberland's technique in politics was genuinely inspired. His trick was to treat Edward seriously, for by the autumn of 1551 the boy was 14 and in the final year of his formal education. It is exaggerating to say that Northumberland and his allies sought to turn him into 'an articulate puppet' whose strings they pulled. But their pretence was that Edward was no longer a minor—and he certainly was no cipher by the time he was 15, but an opinionated teenager determined to hunt, joust, and excel in war exactly like his father.

The subtlety of the Duke's approach, however, was that—just as Henry VIII had been said to be a second King David or King Solomon or a second Emperor Constantine—Edward was said to be a second King Josiah (Figure 7). No more than a boy himself when he had succeeded to the throne, the Old Testament Josiah had purged Judah and Jerusalem of idolatry and reinstituted 'the book of the law' in the temple at Jerusalem. Significantly, Josiah's attack on idolatry had been less the work

The labels within the woodcut read:

The Ship of the Romiſh Church.

Burning of Images.

¶ Ship ouer your trinkets & be packing you Papiſtes.

The Temple well purged.

The Papiſtes packing away their Paltry.

The cōmunion Table.

7. A woodcut designed in 1570 for an enlarged edition of John Foxe's *Acts and Monuments* (or 'Book of Martyrs') to illustrate the swing to Protestantism in the reign of Edward VI, whom the Protestants hailed as a second 'King Josiah'

of the young king himself than of his 'godly councillors' acting in his name. It was a lesson that Northumberland and his ally Archbishop Cranmer, Edward's godfather, purposefully set out to replicate, casting themselves and their fellow privy councillors in the role.

As the man closest to the king after his schoolmaster, John Cheke, Archbishop Cranmer was in a position where he could influence Edward to a degree that even the teenager himself could not fully appreciate. By now, Cranmer's religious beliefs had moved well beyond those of the older generation of evangelical reformers and come closer to those of the mainstream of the Swiss Reformation. And it was to this more radical version of the Reformation that Cranmer and Northumberland meant to convert the king, excluding the traditionalists in religion as far as possible from power.

In 1551–2, Northumberland unleashed Cranmer to overhaul the liturgy that Somerset had botched. A large number of Protestant refugees had settled in London after Charles V's victory over the forces of the Schmalkaldic League at the battle of Mühlberg in 1547. For the very first time, England was seen to be a sanctuary for the reformers, several of whom, such as Peter Martyr Vermigli and Martin Bucer, were Cranmer's friends.

In this volatile, intoxicating atmosphere, Cranmer began canvassing a template for a fully reformed theology of the Eucharist. The debate was rooted in a statement of faith achieved in 1549 between John Calvin and Heinrich Bullinger, which healed the rift between French- and German-speaking Protestants in Switzerland and was known as the *Consensus Tigurinus*. The consultation was then widened to include reformist courtiers and their opponents. In October and November 1551, they thrashed out their differences at the London houses of two of Northumberland's officials, William Cecil and Richard Moryson, leading in 1552 to a second Book of Common Prayer, which affirmed Christ's spiritual presence in the Eucharist only to the elect believer, and so was unambiguously Protestant.

More cynically, Northumberland sent in fresh cohorts of commissioners to all 8,500 parish churches to compile inventories of their wealth. A pressing problem for him was that his revaluation of the coinage had completely drained the royal treasuries of bullion. In desperation, the Privy Council ordered the seizure of all the valuables possessed by the parish churches, 'for as much as the King's Majesty had need presently of a mass of money'.

Nothing was taken until January 1553, but then everything of value went, except for linen, communion vessels, and bells. All gold and silver plate was to be sent to the Jewel House in the Tower of London to be melted down for use in the Royal Mint, and jewels ripped from liturgical vestments were to be stored in coffers there. Cash raised locally from the sale of lesser items was to be sent to the Treasurer of the Mint. So dire was the bullion shortage that plate from St George's Chapel, Windsor, where the Knights of the Garter held their annual procession and feast, was melted down for coin. Jewels and precious metals were even stripped off the bindings of the books in the royal library.

Edward VI's 'device for the succession' and the brief reign of Jane Grey

In April 1552, Edward—who had previously enjoyed robust health—suffered a severe attack of measles. Then, in February 1553, he caught a feverish cold. With his immune system gravely weakened by the measles, he succumbed either to tuberculosis or to bronchopneumonia leading to pleural empyema. Advised by his physicians that his condition was potentially fatal, the teenager convinced himself (or was convinced by Northumberland) that his half-sisters should be excluded from the succession. At this stage, he found unthinkable the notion that a woman might succeed him. Since his father's Parliaments had declared both Mary and Elizabeth illegitimate and those verdicts had never been reversed, Edward came to believe that both were legally barred from the succession.

Religion, however, was the main driving force. Edward, whom Cranmer had converted to his own more advanced Protestant beliefs, did not trust either of his siblings not to dismantle or modify his new Protestant settlement. When sketching out his ideas in early April, he assumed that, before his death, Lady Frances Brandon—whose husband, Henry Grey, had been created Duke of Suffolk in 1551 and whose children were still the next in line to the throne after the king's half-sisters by the terms of

Henry VIII's will—might have a son or that her eldest daughter, Lady Jane Grey (Figure 8), educated by her tutors as a zealous Protestant, might marry and have a son.

Since Lady Frances was approaching the menopause, the more credible prospect was that Jane would marry and that her son

8. An unknown woman, said to be Lady Jane Grey shortly after her marriage to Guildford Dudley. The 'ANO XVIII' (i.e., 'anno aetatis xviii') inscription presents a difficulty in that Jane was not quite 17 when she was executed; however, such inscriptions are not always reliable

(in Edward's eyes) would be the rightful heir. In late May 1553, Northumberland therefore married his 19-year-old son, Guildford Dudley, to the 16-year-old Jane, greatly strengthening his hold on the dynasty because Edward had the highest regard for Guildford, once describing him to the councillors standing around his bedside as 'a man, unless I am mistaken, born to achieve celebrity; from him you may expect great things.'

By June, Edward knew that he was dying. With no time to call Parliament, he put aside his scruples about female monarchy and 'devised' the crown 'to the L[ady] Jane and her heirs male', followed by her sisters and their male heirs, and finally by the eldest son of their cousin Margaret Clifford, daughter of Lady Eleanor Brandon.

The king's death on 6 July 1553 was followed by a hiatus lasting four days while Northumberland took control of the Tower and the royal treasury and swore the head officers of the royal household and the guard to an oath of loyalty to Queen Jane. On the 10th, the heralds proclaimed Jane queen and she took up residence in the royal apartments at the Tower. There she was handed the crown jewels, but she had scarcely received them when her husband Guildford arrived and demanded to be king. A furious row erupted between them, during which Jane reportedly told her husband that he could only be a duke.

First said to have been told by Northumberland's eldest daughter that she was queen, Jane had wept, but prayed to God that, 'If what was given to me was rightly mine, His Divine Majesty would grant me such grace as to enable me to govern this Kingdom with his approbation and to his glory.' Many writers over the centuries have depicted Jane as innocent and manipulated, but once made aware of the contents of Edward's 'Device', she believed that she had been called by God to lead the Protestant cause.

Jane's reign ended abruptly on the 19th, after Henry VIII's elder daughter Mary, the lawful successor according to her father's will, led a swift and effective counter-coup. Warned early of her half-brother's lapse into unconsciousness, she had reacted decisively, riding to the heartland of her estates in Norfolk and from there to Framlingham Castle in Suffolk to muster her forces. The Privy Council sent Northumberland with an army to confront her, but the Duke was deeply unpopular in East Anglia for his role in suppressing the 'stirs' and risings of 1549 and for his confiscation of church goods. When a naval squadron sent to cut off Mary from the Continent defected and handed over its artillery to her, his troops melted away.

By late July, the privy councillors not directly linked by ties of allegiance to Northumberland had all changed sides and disowned him, enabling Mary to recover the capital and the Tower of London. Jane, stripped of the crown jewels and her canopy of state, was escorted from the royal apartments and lodged at the house of William Partridge, an officer in the royal ordnance within the Tower. There, on 29 August, the anonymous author of the *Chronicle of Queen Jane*, the most vivid and authentic account of the events of 1553–4, had dinner with her. Sitting in the place of honour 'at the board's end', she made him welcome and asked for news of the outside world, before launching into a stinging attack on Northumberland, whom Mary had just beheaded, vehemently denouncing him as the source of all her troubles.

Guildford and Jane were tried for treason on 13 November at the London Guildhall. They pleaded guilty and both were sentenced to death. But Mary, although taking her revenge on Northumberland and his closest co-conspirators, was inclined to pity Jane and her brash young husband until faced with Sir Thomas Wyatt's rebellion in January 1554. Wyatt, whose forces reached the gates of London before they were defeated, aimed to overthrow Mary and replace her with her half-sister Elizabeth. After that, Mary considered it was far too dangerous to leave Jane and Guildford alive, and early on the morning of Monday, 12 February, they were beheaded.

Chapter 5
Philip and Mary: An experiment in dual monarchy

The problems of female rule

Acceding to the throne at the age of 37, Mary was England's first female ruler to reign for more than nine days. Apart from Jane Grey, the country had never before known a woman ruler, because Matilda—King Henry I's daughter to whom he had tried to bequeath the crown in 1135—had been forced to flee from London on the eve of her coronation. She had believed she had a lawful dynastic right to succeed, but a woman was not acceptable to the (male) barons and she lost the throne to her cousin Stephen, leading to a long and bitter civil war.

This meant that the pressure was on Mary from the outset and she had never coped well with stress. Once the euphoria at her recovery of the throne was over, her advisers—a mixture of her household retainers, co-religionists, and those privy councillors not closely associated with Northumberland or Jane Grey—attempted to push through an unprecedented measure to have her claim to the throne confirmed by Parliament before she could be crowned.

Always a staunch Catholic, Mary was firmly committed to the ideal of dynastic monarchy and was determined to marry Philip, son of her cousin Charles V. Himself ruling Spain as regent after

1551, Philip would succeed (as Philip II) to the sovereignty of Spain, the Netherlands, and the Spanish-Habsburg lands in Italy and the New World while Mary was still alive. Although it became a central plank of the Protestant platform against her, Mary's marriage offered many advantages. By marrying early in her reign, she could expect to deflect the attacks of those who opposed female rule on principle, while her desire, unfulfilled in the event, to have children was an important signal that she took her duty as a dynastic monarch seriously.

Of all the available prospects, Philip was by far the most eligible spouse: the English candidates for Mary's hand were the obscure scions of noble families and the very notion of marriage to a subject was potentially divisive. Up until now, England's diplomatic and commercial interests had generally been best served by a pro-Habsburg and pro-Netherlandish foreign policy. Overall, there is no reason to suppose that Mary's marriage and her Catholicism, by themselves, were insuperable obstacles to her success. But she and her husband felt insulted and humiliated when Parliament was so opposed to plans for Philip's coronation that no formal proposal was ever laid before it. Fearing that England would be more likely to be dragged into a European war or absorbed into the territorial hegemony of the Habsburgs if Philip was crowned, members of both Lords and Commons believed that a coronation had to be denied.

The nature of the Marian dual monarchy

Mary's wedding was celebrated at Winchester Cathedral on St James's Day (25 July) 1554. According to the marriage treaties, Philip was to be king during Mary's lifetime and the monarchy became, for all practical purposes, a dual monarchy (Figure 9). That said, Philip had no independent rights to the Crown should Mary die. He was not to exercise rights of patronage independently of his wife nor was he to take Mary or any of their future children abroad without Parliament's consent.

9. Philip and Mary as King and Queen of England. Although dated
1558 and apparently set at the palace of Whitehall, the date cannot be
correct since Philip left England in July 1557, never to return. The view
through the open window of the opposite bank of the Thames also
appears to be fictional

Legislation was then passed attempting to limit Philip's rights as a husband and to prescribe that Mary should remain as much 'solely and sole queen' after her marriage as she had been before it. But almost as soon as he arrived in England, Philip was accorded precedence. Official documents styled the monarchs: 'Philip and Mary by the grace of God King and Queen of England, France, Naples, Jerusalem and Ireland; Defenders of the Faith; Princes of Spain and Sicily…'. And at official functions, such as the ceremonies of the Order of the Garter at Windsor, Philip was soon acting as king and sovereign on his own account, a pattern imitated in the wider iconography of the monarchy.

Whether, then, Philip was merely 'king consort' or had become straightforwardly a king in his own right was ambiguous from the beginning, and became increasingly so. Only when he was absent from the country in Brussels or elsewhere did Mary resume her 'sole' authority as ruler. His itinerary thus became crucial. First present in England between July 1554 and early September 1555, and on his second stay between March and July 1557, Philip was absent for the remainder of the reign. It was far from clear, however, that Mary was 'sole' queen while he was not in England, as she paid an almost obsessive attention to discovering his wishes while he was away. And after his first departure in 1555, the issue of 'absentee' monarchy began to filter onto the political agenda, which suggests an expectation that he ought properly to return if he were adequately to fulfil his role.

The Court of Philip and Mary

Philip was accorded his own royal household. The queen's household was located in what, during her father's and brother's reigns, was the part of the royal palaces usually known as 'the king's side'. Philip and his entourage occupied what had formerly been the queen's (or consort's) apartments, but at the leading palace of Whitehall, these had originally been Cardinal Wolsey's apartments, and were actually grander and more spacious than the rooms on Mary's side of the Court.

Whereas Mary's household was relatively small, Philip's must have had difficulty in accommodating itself within the available space. The king brought a full chamber staff with him from Spain only to find another waiting for him in England, complete with a guard of a hundred archers. A compromise was reached that Philip should use Spaniards almost exclusively in his Privy Chamber, leaving his English servants to perform outer chamber and ceremonial duties.

And with Philip soon taking the lead on spending decisions at the royal palaces, there was a confident, unreserved commitment to magnificence and the 'imagination' of majesty on behalf of the dual monarchs. Outdoor events and indoor entertainments were staged on a scale that was as dramatic and impressive as many of Henry VIII's ceremonies, carefully choreographed to project the profile of the dual monarchy. At the opening of Parliament, masses and ornate processions were held involving Spanish as well as English noblemen and courtiers. And to commemorate the deaths of Philip's grandmother Juana of Castile in 1555 and of King John III of Portugal in 1557, elaborate requiem masses were said.

At Juana's requiem, for example, the Spanish and English nobility led the solemn procession into Old St Paul's, walking side by side. There followed the imperial, French, Venetian, and Portuguese ambassadors, the clergy, and a small army of mourners carrying banners and escutcheons decorated with gold and silver. A magnificent hearse was constructed of wax over a timber frame with an ornamental dome and gilded canopy. Wax alone for the four staff torches that surrounded the hearse weighed 1,231 lbs, and the event was reminiscent of no lesser an event than Henry VIII's funeral.

A comprehensive renovation of the furnishings and dynastic symbolism in use at Court was likewise set in train. Large sums from money coined at the Tower Mint by Philip from imported Spanish bullion were partly spent on embroidered cloths of estate, canopies, wall-hangings, heraldic achievements, and badges and accoutrements, all decorated with the initial letters of the king's and queen's names. In the royal stables, fresh horses were purchased—especially the geldings and palfreys beloved of the Spanish courtiers and their wives—and equipped with pommels of gold and silver. A new royal barge, emblazoned in silver and gold and with elaborate wainscoting, was also commissioned and trimmed with the king and queen's regalia.

Philip's role in government

It has often been supposed that Philip had no active role in government—this is pure myth. His role in politics was unquestioned. As soon as he arrived in England, the Lord Privy Seal, then the elderly John Russell, Earl of Bedford, was instructed to 'tell the king the whole state of the Realm, with all things appertaining to the same, as much as ye know to be true' and to answer questions on any matter Philip wished to discuss 'as becometh a faithful councillor to do'. Again, two days after the royal marriage was celebrated at Winchester, the Privy Council issued standing orders to its clerks that 'a note of all such matters of estate as should pass from hence should be made in Latin or Spanish from henceforth, and the same to be delivered to such as it should please the king's highness to appoint to receive it'. State documents of any significance were to be signed by both the king and queen, and a stamp was to be made of both their names for the expedition of lesser matters.

By 1554, an inner circle of councillors associated with crown policy-making had emerged, but the circle was not co-extensive with the members or most regular attendees at Privy Council meetings. On the contrary, its political weight was derived solely from the relationship of individuals to the king and queen. Varying in composition, the circle would soon regularly include Cardinal Pole, whom Pope Julius III named as his plenipotentiary legate to accomplish the reconciliation of England with Rome, and whom Mary appointed archbishop of Canterbury. Pole would became a linchpin of the inner circle after his arrival from Rome, exerting massive influence on secular as well as religious affairs, even though he was never a privy councillor. In fact, he was advising Mary by correspondence on the plans for the reunion with Rome from the moment the queen overthrew Lady Jane Grey.

As if to crystallize this inner circle, a new tier of government was established on the eve of Philip's first departure from England. This was the so-called 'Select Council' or 'Council of State', a council which was of a distinctively European (and Habsburg) type. Spanish-Habsburg practice worked on the basis of regional councils for Castile, Aragon, the Indies, and so on, and departmental councils for war, finance, and the Inquisition, above which sat a policy-making Council of State. It was this last type of council that Philip now envisaged. Its members were to reside at Court and to consider 'all causes of state and financial causes, and other causes of great moment'. They were to report to Philip three times a week, and to brief the other councillors on Sundays.

Thereafter, a regular (and revealing) correspondence between the Select Council and Philip on the business of the realm ensued, beginning with four comprehensive reports submitted by the Council to Philip in Brussels in September 1555. Although the Select Council did not report to Philip as often as it was meant to, it kept him abreast of the affairs of state almost continuously until the end of the reign. Its reports typically dealt with between three and a dozen subjects. Sometimes the original reports were returned to London with Philip's annotations, or else topics were dealt with in correspondence under separate cover. Either way, Philip meticulously studied the Select Council's reports. He sought or received their advice on a wide range of matters: legislation, patronage, and appointments, the nomination and recall of ambassadors, the condition of the regions, the coinage, the appointment of commissioners for tax collection and other social and economic matters, the disputes of foreign merchants, the defence of the realm (especially Portsmouth, Calais, and the Isle of Wight), the activities of English (Protestant) exiles abroad, the state of the borderlands, and relations with Ireland and Scotland.

By the summer of 1556, Philip was anxious about threats of domestic revolt and French invasion. The Select Council wrote to reassure him, and the Earl of Sussex and other nobles and captains were sent to reside in their shires and to take charge of the coastal defences. When reports were received of a general mobilization in France and of naval preparations at Dieppe, the Earl of Pembroke was despatched to Calais to assume command of the town and its security.

All this shows that Philip was not merely a figurehead or even a 'king consort' following his marriage to Mary. He was, and consistently acted as, a reigning king of England, even if he was increasingly absent from the realm.

Marian Counter-Reformation

Mary's evil reputation as a religious persecutor, 'Bloody Mary', would be cemented by John Foxe's *Acts and Monuments* (or 'Book of Martyrs'), published in multiple editions in Elizabeth I's reign and illustrated with gruesome woodcuts. The embers from those fires still smoulder, because any civilized person since the Enlightenment knows that burning people alive for their religious opinions is morally and profoundly wrong. In Mary's lifetime, however, both sides of the confessional divide regarded capital punishment as a legitimate means of enforcing religious conformity.

Mary, who had learned her Catholic faith as a child from her mother, Katherine of Aragon, had her heart set on reversing her father's break with Rome, which after several false starts was achieved in the third Parliament of the reign. We should, however, beware of the bias of Foxe and his fellow Protestant polemicists, who would prefer us to believe that Mary did nothing but persecute. True, Mary and Pole bear the burden of responsibility for the persecution: Philip, notably, opposed it. Although a devoted Catholic himself, he was sceptical of the policy, believing that it would prove counter-productive (as it did)—but on this matter he was content to defer to Pole.

Between them, Mary and Pole burned a minimum of 284 persons after February 1555, and others died in prison. Geographically, the executions were concentrated on London, the South-East, and eastern counties—this for the simple reason that Protestantism was still barely entrenched outside these areas. It is worth mentioning, however, that many of the victims would almost certainly have been burned as radical Protestants under Henry VIII too. And the more prominent martyrs, notably Bishops Hooper, Ridley, and Latimer, and Archbishop Cranmer, were as much the victims of straightforward political vengeance as of religious zeal. What was so exceptional about Mary's 'reign of terror' by contemporary standards was that so many deaths occurred within such a relatively short space of time (between February 1555 and November 1558) and that Pole conscripted a cohort of Spanish Dominicans to assist with the campaign, making it seem as if he had extended the Spanish Inquisition to England.

Whether the campaign was legal continues to be debated. Many of the victims were young. Three-quarters of those whose ages can be discovered had reached the age of spiritual discretion—14 years— after Henry VIII's break with Rome. They were, therefore, not technically heretics, since, if they had never known or received instruction in the true Catholic faith, they could not have renounced it. In particular, the law required that it was not simple doctrinal error or genuine ignorance that was punishable, but 'obstinate' heresy. By this standard, several of the burnings were illegal according to church law itself.

In her defence, Mary's true goal was always reconciliation with Rome—she regarded persecution purely as a means to an end. It worked greatly to her advantage that Philip in 1554 had persuaded the pope to exempt all those who had purchased ex-monastic or chantry lands from returning them to the Church. Mary and Pole, for their part, considered this arrangement to be little short of sacrilege, but, because of it, the landowners in Parliament agreed to repeal the Henrician and Edwardian religious legislation almost without comment.

With these repeals passed, some 800 or so Protestants fled abroad to safe havens in Germany or Switzerland, from where their leaders launched a relentless torrent of subversive literature against Mary. In *A Short Treatise of Politike Power* (1556), John Ponet considered the case of a ruler who had inflicted injuries on his people, arguing that he or she was publicly accountable and could be punished as a criminal. Christopher Goodman's *How Superior Powers Ought to be Obeyed of their Subjects*, published in January 1558, went further, claiming that the wicked Catholic queen was 'a bastard by birth' and a 'traitor to God', a tyrant who could be deposed and killed.

A similar line was taken by the fiery Scottish preacher, John Knox, who had lived in England in Edward's reign when he served as one of the young king's chaplains. His *First Blast of the Trumpet against the Monstrous Regiment of Women*, published in the spring of 1558, was a sensational diatribe against female rule, claiming that a Catholic woman ruler was 'a monster in nature' and unfit to rule on grounds of religion and gender. By publicly embracing undiluted Protestantism in 1552, declared Knox, England had entered into a covenant with God which bound its elected magistrates in Parliament to depose and destroy an idolatrous ruler.

Pole, meanwhile, tried his best to introduce church reform on Catholic lines. Unflinching and determined, he began to found seminaries for the recruitment and education of new clergy, to rejuvenate preaching and the liturgy, and to take steps more generally to raise standards of everyday ministry in the parishes. His measures place him firmly in the vanguard of the Counter-Reformation—Spanish Dominicans were even sent to Oxford to galvanize change. But his approach was also visionary and impersonal. He saw people not as individuals but as a multitude, and he emphasized unduly the need for discipline, seeking to be an 'indulgent' pastor who relieved his flock of choices they were too foolish to make for themselves. Dubbing himself the 'Pole Star', he thought his mere presence on the scene could guide lost souls. His reforms might have succeeded in the end, but it would have taken a generation or more to bed them in.

Financial reforms

The regime secured quicker and longer lasting results in the sphere of Crown finance. Partly financed by the imported silver bullion that Philip converted at the Tower Mint into around £40,000-worth of English coin (£40 million in modern values), the currency was stabilized and the fiscal reforms begun by Northumberland brought nearer to completion. A system of regular audits was introduced, and the Exchequer was revitalized and reorganized by merging several other revenue and accounting departments with it.

To increase income, royal debtors were pursued and a revaluation of the crown lands undertaken to compensate for the inroads made by inflation on rents and entry fines. Concealments of land belonging to the Crown were investigated and tighter controls applied to leasing policy. Since customs duties had not been increased since 1507, a new Book of Rates was introduced in 1558 that raised duties on average by 100 per cent and placed a new levy on cloth exports.

Moreover, to pave the way for levying parliamentary taxes with greater frequency, Philip and Mary developed an idea first tried as an experiment by Thomas Cromwell in 1534, which justified taxes in and after 1555 on the assumption that taxpayers should assume responsibility for a national budget indexed regularly in relation to inflation and population figures to meet the normal costs of government. Historically, direct taxation had only been judged by Parliament to be acceptable in cases of war or emergency, such as revolts. Taxpayers expected the Crown to finance the regular costs of peacetime government itself out of its ordinary land revenues or customs duties, which was unrealistic. When Cromwell had run his experiment in 1534, it had contributed significantly to the risings of 1536–7, so it had not been tried since.

Had the more aggressive fiscal planning of the Marian era been carried to its logical conclusion, many of the fiscal problems of Elizabeth I might have been averted. But this would not happen, since Elizabeth would prove herself to be a conservative where taxation was concerned.

Mary's pseudo-pregnancy

Mary believed herself to be pregnant in the winter of 1554–5. Her half-sister Elizabeth took the reports seriously enough to ask the astrologer John Dee to cast a series of royal horoscopes. The 'destinies' she tried to have foreseen were her own, Philip's, and Mary's. Casting a royal horoscope was a dangerous, potentially treasonable business—the fact that Elizabeth took the risk shows how genuine she believed the reports to be.

At the end of March 1555, Mary was so convinced that she was 'near her time', she chose Hampton Court as the place where she would take to her lying-in chamber. Royal women were expected to retreat into total seclusion when they prepared to have their baby, moving into a special, blacked-out chamber with only one window open to the light and attended only by their gentlewomen and the midwife. So confident was Mary, however, that God was on her side, that she broke protocol, leaning out of her window to show herself to Philip and his fellow Knights of the Garter as they processed in their robes to Chapel on St George's Day (23 April). Not just was she overconfident about her pregnancy, she was convinced she would have a son. On 16 May, she and Philip actually began signing open letters to foreign princes announcing 'the happy delivery of a prince' and appointing special messengers to deliver them.

Unfortunately, no child was born. Mary was suffering from a pseudo-pregnancy, complete with a swelling of the breasts and lactation. Philip had placed all his hopes on the birth of a child—when in August it became clear that the pregnancy was a phantom, the royal couple returned to Whitehall scarcely on speaking terms. When on 4 September Philip sailed from Dover to Calais on his way back to Brussels, his departure marked a watershed, for he would not return until March 1557, and only then to drag England into an unpopular war against France.

Realizing she had been all but deserted, Mary succumbed to fits of hysterics, on one occasion haranguing Philip's portrait hanging in the Privy Chamber before kicking it out of the room. Relations between the couple swiftly deteriorated. Mary felt it to be her Christian (and political) duty to obey her husband in all matters on which he offered her advice, and she several times wrote to him to seek his opinion. Despite this, on many occasions she acceded to his will through gritted teeth.

War and opposition to the regime

It was Mary's misfortune that her rule coincided with some of the sharpest and most severe economic and demographic spikes for half a century. Harvest failures and a severe dearth in 1555–7 caused malnutrition and some starvation. When an influenza epidemic struck in 1556, the death rate soared. This proved to be the most serious mortality crisis since the Black Death in 1348: the population dropped by more than 200,000—6 per cent—in three years. Rumours of sedition and conspiracy were rife. They included reports of putative or failed assassination attempts, claims that Edward VI was still alive and stories that Mary had given birth to a monster.

Fears of revolt were not unjustified. In 1554, the regime and the London citizens had been shaken by Sir Thomas Wyatt's rebellion. A second conspiracy, known as the Ashton-Dudley plot, was planned in Elizabeth's favour in 1556 by a Berkshire gentleman, Christopher Ashton, and a military man, Sir Harry Dudley, the Duke of Northumberland's fourth cousin. Aiming to rob the Exchequer of £50,000, the conspirators planned to fund an army of mercenaries and Protestant exiles who would invade England, drive out the Spaniards, and depose Mary.

Part of the plot involved handing Calais to the French, and when the plan was betrayed, Mary was determined to put all those implicated in it on trial for treason. Key military officials, such as the captain of Yarmouth Castle, were implicated, as were some leading Protestant gentry. A recurrent theme of the conspiracy was continuing opposition to Philip's coronation. The plan was sketchy and relied almost entirely on luck and opportunity, but came surprisingly close to success.

Opposition to the regime peaked in March 1557, when Philip sought England's assistance in the Spanish-Habsburg invasion of France. Pressure from Philip, and later from Mary herself, ensured that a highly unpopular decision to enter the war was finally taken. Hostilities were declared on 7 June 1557. At first the campaign went well. An important victory was won at St Quentin, but, at home, the battle was overshadowed by the costs and dangers incurred. Mutual trust between Philip and the Privy Council collapsed after the king's second and final departure in July 1557.

When the greatest humiliation of the reign, the loss of Calais, occurred on 1 January 1558, the recriminations were bitter. The town was the last of the former possessions of Henry V that had remained in English hands. It was attacked by 27,000 French troops who advanced across the frozen marshes: the failures of the English defences had been culpable. The loss of Calais paralysed the regime; the morale of the Select Council collapsed. Only Pole continued to enjoy Philip's confidence.

Reports of Mary's second pseudo-pregnancy, meanwhile, turned her into something close to a laughing-stock. Some of her own trusted servants lampooned her, while in France, Charles, Cardinal of Lorraine, one of the Guise uncles of the young Mary, Queen of Scots, unkindly quipped that she would not have long to wait, 'this being the end of the eighth month since her husband left her'. Mary was suffering from a serious, undiagnosed illness, possibly a prolactinoma, a non-cancerous tumour of the pituitary gland which causes pseudo-pregnancies and the other symptoms from which she suffered—migraines, depression, and the onset of blindness.

Mary's death in November 1558 was mourned only by her closest friends and Catholic supporters, and the fact that Pole died within a few hours of her seemed to the Protestants to be an act of divine providence. King Henry II of France, meanwhile, exulted with *Te Deum* and bonfires, and the marriage of Mary Stuart, Queen of Scots, to the Dauphin—the perilous consequence of the aggression of Henry VIII and Protector Somerset—was put in hand.

Chapter 6
The early Elizabethan polity

Elizabeth's accession

Elizabeth I, the 25-year-old daughter of Henry VIII and Anne Boleyn, ascended her throne on Thursday, 17 November 1558. The transition was peaceful, but the new queen could have no expectation that this would be so. On the contrary, Mary—like her half-brother before her—had actively considered excluding her from the succession until Philip, who had once considered marrying Elizabeth himself, stepped in to protect his young sister-in-law. Philip now had plans to marry elsewhere, but he believed that if he handled Elizabeth in the right way, he could continue to influence her and perhaps draw England gradually back within a Spanish-Habsburg orbit. He was unsure about her religion, since in Mary's reign—and especially at dangerous moments—she had conformed, if reluctantly, to the mass.

On hearing that Mary was dying, Philip had sent the Count of Feria, one of his leading councillors, to salvage what Spanish interests he could. In a relatively brief audience, Feria, who reported Elizabeth to be 'a very vain and clever woman', grasped some of the reasons for her future success as a ruler: she could keep her nerve in a crisis. She also put 'great store' by the people, whom she 'is very confident...are on her side'. It was the people, she had insisted, 'who put her in her present position' and—as

Feria warned Philip—'she will not acknowledge that Your Majesty or the nobility of this realm had any part in it'.

Elizabeth had (with rare exceptions) a surefooted ability to gauge public opinion and was a natural orator. She understood the power of words and knew how important a part they played in politics—not least in the Council chamber and Parliament. One of her favourite quotations from classical literature was from the first oration of Isocrates to Nicocles, the young king of Cyprus. It ran, 'Throughout all your life show that you value truth so highly that a king's word is more to be trusted than other men's oaths.'

That said, she could sometimes appear just as distant, aloof, imperious, and vindictive as her father. A strong ruler, she none the less found it necessary on a dozen or so occasions to take a stand when her councillors, ambassadors, or military commanders refused or were reluctant to obey her—more than one would express their extreme frustration at taking orders they disliked 'from a mere woman'. Had Elizabeth been a man, she could have expected to be obeyed without question. As it was, her chief councillor, Sir William Cecil, on the one hand, called her 'the commander', and yet, on the other, there were some spectacular examples of his determination to subvert or modify her instructions to suit his own priorities.

Cecil was with Elizabeth on the day Mary died, functioning as the new queen's Secretary of State. He had been in her service since 1549, when she had sent him a message that shows he was already her Court agent. He had become the surveyor of her estates in 1550. And as the Duke of Northumberland's secretary and a privy councillor in Edward's reign, and again while his career was on hold in Mary's reign, he had worked with Elizabeth's household servants to protect her and safeguard her interests. True, there had been a glitch, because Cecil had assisted Lady Jane Grey and almost certainly served briefly as her Secretary of State, even though he later denied so close an association. His defence would doubtless have been 'necessity' and the need to defend the Protestant cause. Despite this, his political partnership with Elizabeth, for all its ups and downs, was rock solid and would last until Cecil's death in 1598.

The religious settlement

The first steps of the new regime were to reverse Mary's reunion of England with Rome and secure a religious settlement more enduring than Edward's. Elizabeth's personal credo remains elusive, but it seems likely that she was a moderate Protestant, one whose evangelical beliefs were closer to those of her stepmother, Katherine Parr, than to those of many of her own supporters. It appears that she originally aimed to re-establish the royal supremacy and the break with Rome, and to permit communion in both kinds (the bread and the wine) after the reformed fashion, but nothing else. If so, this was one of the occasions when she was outmanoeuvred, because Cecil—a Protestant more deeply attuned to the doctrines set out by the Swiss reformers in the *Consensus Tigurinus* and a known ally of those who had fled into exile in Mary's reign—aimed to achieve a settlement based on that made by Archbishop Cranmer and the Duke of Northumberland in 1552.

When Parliament assembled in January 1559, Cecil and Francis Russell, the new Earl of Bedford—another noted advocate of Lady Jane Grey and a former exile—introduced bills to re-establish the royal supremacy and full Protestant worship based on Cranmer's 1552 Prayer Book. And when these were resolutely opposed by the former Marian bishops and remaining Catholic peers, Cecil baited a trap. A disputation was begun at Westminster Abbey (31 March) which restricted debate to what was justified by Scripture alone. When the Catholics walked out, Cecil had a propaganda victory: two bishops were even imprisoned.

To ease the passage of the bills through Parliament, Elizabeth was styled 'Supreme Governor' and not 'Supreme Head' of the

English Church in an effort to minimize the implications of sacral monarchy for a woman. The Elizabethan Settlement was completed in 1563, when Convocation approved Thirty-nine Articles defining the Church of England's doctrine: these were based on 42 drafted by Cranmer late in Edward's reign. In 1571, the settlement gained teeth sharper than the new Acts of Supremacy and Uniformity when a Subscription Act required all beneficed clergy to assent to the Thirty-nine Articles or else resign.

Despite its many faults and ambiguities, the new national Church spared England from the Wars of Religion that would soon cripple other European states. And yet, while the settlement officially made England Protestant, a huge missionary effort lay ahead to win over the hearts and minds of parishioners in the remoter shires and borderlands.

The decline of Catholicism over the coming years was due partly to mortality. Before 1571, over 225 Marian priests were still active in Yorkshire and Lancashire, the chief centres of mass Catholic recusancy. By 1590, however, barely a quarter of these were still alive, and no more than a dozen by 1603.

At first, the survival of Catholic dissent was helped by the spasmodic nature of Elizabeth's drive for conformity. In the 1560s, Catholics were rarely persecuted if they kept their heads down. This was not least if they shut their eyes and ears to what was going on around them and attended the official church services occasionally. As someone who had conformed to the mass herself in the past when forced to do so by her half-sister, it was hardly fitting that Elizabeth should pry into the private beliefs of her subjects, as long as they offered 'outward conformity' to her settlement.

Only Pope Pius V's decision in 1570 to issue a bull entitled *Regnans in Excelsis*, excommunicating the queen and calling on her Catholic subjects to depose her, led to a campaign of persecution. In 1571, Parliament enacted new treason legislation, and when the threat of a Catholic invasion from Spain dramatically increased in 1584–5, Parliament declared that if any Catholic priest had been ordained since 1559, he was automatically a traitor—no extra proof was needed. Many priests were savagely racked and manacled in the Tower by men like Richard Topcliffe, a near-psychopath licensed by Cecil, a man whom Elizabeth knew and conversed with, and who sat in Parliament, but of whose existence she always pretended to be ignorant. Almost 150 priests, many ordained abroad, were beheaded or tortured in these later years.

But in the end it was Protestant evangelism, rather than persecution, that succeeded in forcing Catholicism into minority status. Such evangelism was largely based on 'godly' preaching, although Elizabeth's parsimony and own conservative religious views precluded a full government programme. Often more was achieved thanks to voluntary, so-called 'puritan', efforts.

A term of abuse, 'puritan' was used to index the nature and extent of the more radical Protestant opinions of which the queen and the stricter sort of conformists disapproved. The word came to mean a 'church rebel' or 'hotter sort' of Protestant—those especially who had fled to Switzerland in Mary's reign and who regarded the new Church of England as 'but halfly reformed'. But the core of puritan values lay in the capacity of 'godly' and zealous Protestants to recognize each other within a corrupt and unregenerate world. Men of genuine religious passion, the 'puritans' sought to extirpate corruption and 'popish' ceremonies and vestments from the Church (the cross in baptism, the ring in marriage, kneeling at Holy Communion, the wearing of copes and surplices, the use of organs, etc.).

Elizabeth, however, refused to adjust the settlement even in detail. Her invariable habit was to refer petitioners seeking 'further reformation' to the bishops—and if the bishops offered them their support, she simply turned a blind eye to their recommendations.

Faced after 1563 by howls of protests over church vestments, Matthew Parker, the new archbishop of Canterbury, issued *Advertisements* in 1566 that strictly enforced the rubrics of the Prayer Book. When in 1576 his successor Edmund Grindal—a former exile who shared a yearning for 'further reformation'— dared to tell the queen that he was subject to a higher power when she ordered him to reduce the number of 'godly' preachers to no more than three or four for a shire and cease his support for the 'prophesyings' (i.e., preaching conferences led by puritan ministers to educate the more backward clergy), he was suspended from office. Grindal was shocked to discover that so many of the parochial clergy were 'dumb dogs'—unable to preach—and was deeply frustrated that the ministers suspended or dismissed by Parker for their disobedience over church vestments included his own ordinands—men who had preached to wildly enthusiastic crowds in London.

'Remember, Madam, that you are a mortal creature', was just one of several observations Grindal made to Elizabeth. Not even Cecil could salvage his career after that.

Marriage and the succession

Elizabethan politics were dominated for almost 30 years by the issues of the queen's marriage, the Protestant succession, and the threat from Europe and Scotland. In the eyes of the Catholic powers, Elizabeth was unfit to rule as she was a heretic, a bastard, and challenged as to her title and right of succession by Mary, Queen of Scots. For their part, Cecil and his 'assured friends' in the Privy Council and Parliament followed a proactive and surprisingly radical approach to dealing with these problems, an outlook informed by their keen sense of Protestant identity and divine providence.

Faced by Elizabeth's refusal in late 1559 to send an expeditionary force to Scotland to expel the French garrison at Leith and help engineer a Protestant revolution, Cecil threatened to resign until she changed her mind. The revolution was successful and the Catholic regent, Mary of Guise, was deposed. But even before the young Queen of Scots returned as a widow from France to take up her throne in Scotland in August 1561, Cecil—who was later aided by his protégé and spymaster, Sir Francis Walsingham—believed that the forces of darkness, in particular the papacy, Spain, and Mary's Guise relations, were mobilizing against England and that they intended to use Mary as their instrument. Cecil wanted Mary neutralized and, if possible, deposed as Queen of Scots, and he quietly began plotting in 1563 to exclude her from the English succession should Elizabeth fail to marry or have children, just as Edward VI had attempted to exclude his half-sisters.

In July 1561, Cecil wrote to Sir Nicholas Throckmorton, then ambassador in France: 'God send our mistress a husband, and by him a son, that we may hope our posterity shall have a masculine succession.' And in Parliament first in 1563 and again in 1566, Cecil worked tirelessly (and covertly) with his allies (many of them puritans) in an effort to persuade Elizabeth to marry and settle the succession. He worked equally circumspectly (and dangerously) to keep alive the claim to the throne of Katherine Grey, Lady Jane's younger sister, who had enraged Elizabeth by secretly marrying the Earl of Hertford, eldest son of Protector Somerset, by whom she had two sons—this even though Elizabeth had forcibly separated the couple and thrown Katherine into the Tower.

Elizabeth several times promised Parliament that she would marry when the circumstances were right—but they never were. In the first 18 months of the reign, she was in love with Robert Dudley (Figure 10), an elder brother of Guildford, the man who had married Jane Grey. In these months, Robert was rarely absent from Court. The Count of Feria claimed in April 1559, 'Lord Robert has come so much into favour that he does whatever he

10. Robert Dudley, Earl of Leicester, the only man whom Elizabeth truly loved as queen and whose last letter, written shortly before his death in 1588, she lovingly preserved. But their relationship was often turbulent

likes with affairs and it is even said that her Majesty visits him in his chamber day and night'.

By the autumn, their intimacy was a source of salacious gossip, since Robert was already married to Amy Robsart. Despite this, there was talk of marriage and divorce. The scandal broke in September 1560, when news reached the Court that Amy had been found dead at the foot of a small stone spiral staircase while lodged at Cumnor Place, near Oxford. A coroner's jury brought in a verdict of accidental death, but whether Amy fell accidentally or was pushed has never been proved.

Elizabeth hesitated, and then decided that a marriage to Dudley was too dangerous. Only after two years' delay was he admitted to the Privy Council, and he would not be created Earl of Leicester until 1564. Elizabeth retained an enduring affection for her first favourite: she kept his portrait miniature in her closet, and lovingly preserved his last letter, written shortly before his death in 1588. But their relationship was often turbulent, especially when Dudley acted presumptuously—then the queen would humiliate him, and even exile him from Court.

After her fling with Dudley, Elizabeth sought to detach her emotions from political considerations. Her marriage became a mere tool of politics and foreign policy. Her more credible suitors in this phase included King Eric XIV of Sweden, the Archduke Charles of Austria, and Henry, younger brother of King Charles IX of France, who later succeeded to the French throne as King Henry III (1574–89). The Archduke was seriously considered between 1563 and 1567, but the diplomacy collapsed when Cecil found out that he insisted on hearing mass in the queen's household.

The same problem dogged the negotiations with France that began in 1570. Elizabeth pursued the idea of a French match at this stage because she knew she needed to build a defensive alliance against Spain, even though she constantly worried that at 37, and with an age gap of 18 years between them, she was old enough to be the prospective bridegroom's mother. When in 1572 Cecil and Walsingham secured an alliance, regardless of marriage, by the Treaty of Blois, the proposed match was dropped.

None of this denies that Elizabeth might have married if the candidate and the terms had been right. Robert Dudley, the man who knew her best, may have come closest to the truth—for when conversing with the nephew of the French ambassador in 1566, he confided that his 'true opinion was that she would never marry'.

The trouble was that her marriage and the succession were inextricably linked. In a rare, unguarded moment while conversing privately in 1561 with William Maitland of Lethington, Secretary of State to Mary, Queen of Scots, Elizabeth declared emphatically that the Scottish queen had by far the best dynastic claim to succeed her if Elizabeth were to die childless. To Cecil's consternation, it was a view she continued to hold for at least ten more years.

Cecil was determined to make the succession dependent on a religious test rather than on hereditary right. He and his allies were adamant that the next ruler of England should be a Protestant, and not a Catholic. The sense of crisis deepened sharply in 1565, when Mary impulsively married Henry, Lord Darnley, son of the Earl and Countess of Lennox, and grandson of Henry VIII's elder sister Margaret (Figure 11). Worse for Cecil and his 'assured friends', a year later Mary and Darnley had a son, christened James. From now onwards, Cecil worried constantly that 'S.Q.'—'the Scottish Queen', for he could not even bear to speak or write her name—was still alive. For him at least, 'Mary' and 'Scotland' were to a significant degree the organizing principle of Elizabethan politics.

11. Mary, Queen of Scots, with her second husband, Henry, Lord Darnley, whom she married in July 1565, precipitating a noble revolt in Scotland and leading within two years to his brutal assassination

By 1565, there was a sharp ideological rift between Elizabeth and Cecil over Mary and Scottish affairs. Despite their ability to work together over almost every other issue, Elizabeth and her chief minister were at loggerheads where Mary was concerned. Whereas Cecil put Protestantism ahead of hereditary, dynastic rights in debating the succession, Elizabeth took the opposite approach. Although she was a Protestant, she kept religion and politics apart, putting the ideal of monarchy ahead of religion. Mary was herself a great-granddaughter of Henry VII, and after marrying Darnley, she had the best possible claim to the English succession unless Elizabeth herself married and had children.

Elizabeth wanted a settlement with Mary and even agreed to meet her in 1562. Only the massacre of a Huguenot (Protestant) congregation at Vassy by one of Mary's uncles, Francis, Duke of Guise, prevented it. True, she was never willing to identify Mary or anyone else *by name* as her successor. But she was prepared to protect Mary's rights, most sensationally in the winter of 1566–7, when she offered to allow a panel of judges to test the validity and legitimacy of Henry VIII's will, which had relegated the descendants of the king's elder sister Margaret to the status of residuary legatees rather than nominated heirs.

In this tense and ideologically intoxicating atmosphere, Cecil made serious attempts to draft an Exclusion Bill, to exclude the Catholic Mary from the succession forever by Act of Parliament. For this, he can rightly be depicted as a quasi-republican, because his vision of Catholic women rulers was analogous to John Knox's in *The First Blast of the Trumpet against the Monstrous Regiment of Women*. Catholics would soon bitterly lampoon him in an anonymous tract entitled *A Treatise of Treasons against Queen Elizabeth* (*c*.1571–2), accusing him of leading a 'Machiavellian' clique that sought to turn Elizabeth into a puppet queen. He and his 'assured friends', they bitterly complained, pulled the strings to Elizabeth's shame and dishonour: when they had done away with Mary, they would turn on Elizabeth herself.

Elizabeth's refusal to condone Cecil's attempts at exclusion shows the limits of the model depicting Elizabeth and Mary as 'rival' British Queens. Elizabeth certainly wanted to exercise control over her cousin (and to a lesser extent Scotland) and especially to influence (and preferably dictate) whom she married in the interests of her own security and that of the two 'British' realms. But the two queens had far more in common than the model allows.

Unfortunately for Mary, her husband Darnley was a sop, an inveterate schemer, and a serial adulterer, who demanded to be king. When in 1566–7 he fell out dramatically with the Scottish nobles, he was brutally assassinated in a gunpowder plot at Kirk o'Field on the outskirts of Edinburgh. Despite countless allegations to the contrary afterwards, Mary was not involved in the murder, but the choice of husband was the key area in which a female ruler could not afford mistakes if she was to rule successfully. In May 1567, Mary got it badly wrong again, marrying James Hepburn, Earl of Bothwell. And yet, when in the summer of 1567 Mary was imprisoned at Lochleven Castle by her half-brother, James Stuart, Earl of Moray, and forced to abdicate, Elizabeth was genuinely horrified and demanded that she be freed.

When Mary outwitted her gaolers and fled to England in 1568, Elizabeth (on Cecil's stern advice) reluctantly put her under house arrest. A chain of intrigues then took shape in which Catholic, papal, and pro-Spanish ambitions allied threateningly, keeping Cecil at his desk long into the small hours. Luckily for him, a plot to marry Mary to the Duke of Norfolk and a Catholic rebellion in the North (1569) were incoherently attempted and easily crushed. For preserving her throne, Elizabeth in 1571 rewarded Cecil with a promotion to the peerage as Lord Burghley. And by 1572, Elizabeth and Cecil had seemingly triumphed, even if Cecil strived unceasingly to have Mary beheaded rather than simply detained against her will as a queen in exile.

The Protestant cause and the Armada

Mary's flight to England and the Northern Rising marked the onset of a new, more dangerous phase in politics. Throughout Europe, opinion was polarizing on religious grounds: England's role as a Protestant champion was central. Relations with Spain had seriously deteriorated when Cecil seized Philip II's treasure ships on their way to the Netherlands (December 1568). Then Pius V issued the bull *Regnans in Excelsis*, declaring Elizabeth to be excommunicated and deposed. There followed a massacre of the Huguenots in Paris and several provincial towns on St Bartholomew's Day 1572, and outright rebellion in the Netherlands. Since 1566, the Netherlands had been smouldering, for the Dutch Protestants and their allies among the nobles, led by

William of Orange, were in revolt against the sovereignty of Spain and sought to make a common cause with England, the Huguenots, and the German Protestant princes. Their passion and commitment, above all their terrible suffering at the hands of Philip's mighty Army of Flanders, fired Protestant consciences and inspired many Englishmen to volunteer aid to both the Dutch and the Huguenots.

In late 1575, Elizabeth was offered the sovereignty of the provinces of Holland and Zeeland, but as a staunch defender of the ideal of monarchy, she was extremely wary of condoning rebels or accepting the role of protector of Protestantism throughout Europe. She greatly feared that getting involved in costly foreign wars would ruin her finances. She therefore stuck by the defensive alliance with France that Cecil and Walsingham had negotiated in 1572, using it to counter-balance the power of Spain and so offer indirect support and assistance to the Dutch.

On these matters the Privy Council was split, but the divisions were over tactics rather than over fundamental principles. Several councillors feared (as did Elizabeth) that the French aimed to annex or partition the Netherlands and that their overtures to England were a feint. Others, including Cecil, feared the extent to which England could become militarily overextended by intervening abroad. But no one seriously doubted that a dangerous alliance was forming between Spain and the Guise (ultra-Catholic) faction in France, one that posed a terrible threat to Protestants everywhere.

In these difficult circumstances, Elizabeth allowed herself to be wooed by Francis, Duke of Anjou, the younger brother of Henry III of France, in the belief that it might be possible to mould him as a 'Protector of the Netherlands' and so assist the Dutch at minimal cost to herself. When at last Anjou arrived in England in August 1579, she appeared to be a woman in love, despite her fear that his facial appearance (he was badly disfigured by smallpox) and their 21-year age gap would make him a figure of fun. None the less, in June 1581 a marriage treaty was signed, but with the reservation that the religious clauses were to be settled between Elizabeth and Anjou.

When Anjou returned to London in November, Elizabeth 'drew off a ring from her finger, and put it upon the Duke of Anjou's, upon certain conditions betwixt them two'. According to a Spanish report, she even kissed him on the mouth. Was it a genuine romance? How much was real and how much a pretence to guarantee England's security against the growing threat of Catholic Spain?

But no marriage took place. Faced by intense domestic opposition, much of it from within the Privy Council itself, Elizabeth stalled and Anjou died in June 1584, having failed ignominiously to halt Spanish power in the Netherlands. Then, when the Protestant Henry of Navarre became heir to the French throne, the Wars of Religion resumed in France. If anything, the stakes rose ever higher as the Guise faction openly allied with Spain by the secret Treaty of Joinville (December 1584).

The result was that, when war with Spain came in 1585, England would be isolated. For some years, the Marquis of Santa Cruz had been lobbying support in Spain for an 'Enterprise of England', nothing less than a 'Grand Armada' to overthrow Elizabeth as a prelude to the reconquest of the Dutch. Pundits debated only whether the Netherlands or England would crumble first.

The pivotal event was the assassination with a pistol of the Dutch leader, William of Orange (10 July 1584). This created panic among members of the Privy Council who, stirred into action by Cecil and Walsingham, called upon all members of Parliament and local magistrates to sign a Bond of Association in which they pledged to defend Elizabeth's life, and hunt down and kill anyone involved in a plot to assassinate her, whether as a co-conspirator or as the beneficiary of such a plot. The main target of the Bond was Mary, Queen of Scots—once again, Cecil had been influenced by the political ideas of the former Marian exiles.

Elizabeth disapproved of the Bond which she saw as lynch law, but was powerless to stop it. Her councillors were looking to her for decisive leadership, but she found herself increasingly hemmed in by her own indecision. Only when, in May 1585, Philip felt confident enough to seize all English ships in Iberian ports did she know she could delay no longer. She retaliated, allying with the Dutch States General in August and dispatching her favourite Robert Dudley, Earl of Leicester, to Holland with a large expeditionary force.

But Dudley's campaign turned into a fiasco: his humiliating recall would shortly be followed by his death. Only Sir Francis Drake and other naval freebooters would enjoy more or less unqualified success as they raided Spanish ports and intercepted Philip's treasure ships on the high seas. Meanwhile, Catholic plots linked to Spain and the Guise relations of Mary, Queen of Scots, became so threatening that it seemed as if all Cecil's worst nightmares were coming true.

Elizabeth was most consistently indecisive where her Scottish cousin was concerned. Although accused by Walsingham of aiding and abetting Anthony Babington's conspiracy against Elizabeth in 1586 and put on trial, Mary was an anointed queen and Elizabeth repudiated a regicide that was authorized by an act of State. All she would do was grudgingly to encourage Walsingham to arrange that Mary be smothered by her gaolers at dead of night, an act to which the signatories to the Bond of Association had already committed themselves if they could square it with their consciences.

But the Privy Council could wait no longer. Once it became clear that nothing short of a major jolt would budge Elizabeth into signing Mary's death warrant, Cecil lied to her, pretending that another assassination plot had been 'discovered' at the French embassy (it was actually an old plot known for over a year). Cecil even helped to foster a false rumour that the Spanish Armada had landed in Wales.

The result was that Elizabeth signed her cousin's death warrant, but gave orders that it was not to leave her secretary's hands until she gave further instructions. Cecil, however, summoned the Privy Council to a special meeting and—without Elizabeth's knowledge—had the warrant quickly dispatched.

Mary was therefore executed in conditions of the utmost secrecy at Fotheringhay Castle (8 February 1587), this even after Elizabeth had attempted to recall the warrant. Scotland (and Elizabeth herself) fulminated, but the 21-year-old James VI was won over by subsidies and enhanced prospects of the greatest of glittering prizes—succession to the English throne. At last Cecil and his 'assured friends' had got what they wanted and Mary was dead. The problem from Elizabeth's viewpoint was that they had created a legal precedent for regicide.

The Armada was sighted off the Scilly Isles on 19 July 1588 (Figure 12). The Spanish plan was to win control of the English Channel, to rendezvous with the Duke of Parma off the coast of Holland, and then to transport the crack troops of Philip's Army of Flanders to England. There they would unite with the forces already on board the Armada itself in a combined invasion of England.

The key to the main battle, fought off Gravelines on the Flemish coast, was artillery. For reasons of weight and manoeuvrability, the Armada carried only 19 or 20 full cannon, but its 173 medium-heavy guns were ineffective—some exploding on use—which suggests they had not been tested. And whereas the Spanish had only 21 culverins (long-range iron guns), the English had 153;

12. The Spanish Armada, first sighted off the Scilly Isles on 19 July 1588

whereas the Spanish had 151 demi-culverins, the English had 344. In brief, the English commanders led by Lord Howard of Effingham and Sir Francis Drake both out-sailed and out-gunned their opponents.

The battered Armada fled north towards the Firth of Forth, trailing back to Spain via the Orkneys and the west coast of Ireland. In August 1588, the country celebrated with prayers and public thanksgiving. But the escape had been narrow and Elizabeth never again committed her whole fleet in battle at once. Moreover, although later generations boasted that she had kept Spain at bay at minimum cost, by avoiding foreign alliances and relying on the royal navy and part-time privateers who preyed on enemy shipping, the supremacy of the naval over the Continental land war is a myth. The war at sea was only part of a struggle that gripped the whole of Western Europe and centred on the French

Wars of Religion and Dutch revolt. Aligned to Spain were the forces of the Catholic League in France led by the Guise faction. Since Elizabeth lacked the resources to fight them on her own, she was obliged to seek the help of Henry of Navarre and the Dutch. The Catholic League was strongest in Picardy, Normandy, and Brittany. These regions and the Netherlands formed what amounted to a continuous war zone.

Elizabeth, at vast cost, dispatched auxiliary forces annually to France and the Netherlands in 1589–95. In addition, her cash subsidies to the Huguenots and the Dutch, quite apart from the costs of equipping and paying her own troops, amounted to well over £1 million (more than £1 billion in modern values). And casualties were dire—11,000 men were killed in France alone in less than three years. By comparison, English naval operations in the Atlantic and Pacific oceans must have seemed like heroic sideshows. Who could tell if it would all end in disaster?

Chapter 7
Material culture and the arts

Architecture and housing

Under Henry VIII and Wolsey, the art of the Italian Renaissance first permeated the Court circle in a significant way. The shift began when the brilliant and versatile Florentine sculptor Pietro Torrigiano was commissioned to produce the tombs of Margaret Beaufort and of Henry VII and Elizabeth of York. In the 1520s, Wolsey hired more Florentines, notably Benedetto da Rovezzano, to construct his (never finished) tomb and design the high altar of the new college he founded at Oxford. A prodigious builder, who within a decade turned an ordinary manor house at Hampton Court into a palace fit for himself and a king, Wolsey enlarged several of his other houses in the grandest style, while at the same time singlehandedly overseeing Henry VIII's own building operations. When in 1520 the cardinal masterminded the arrangements for the Field of Cloth of Gold, he personally vetted 'the plat' for the design of the English temporary palace, which was famous for its Renaissance style and decorations.

By the 1530s and 1540s, classical and Italian styles had become commonplace as Henry VIII invested heavily in building works and decorations at Whitehall and at Nonsuch Palace in Surrey. In imitation, courtiers routinely embellished their own houses with classically inspired stucco festoons, busts, roundels, cameos, and goldsmiths' work. The trend began in the 1530s with Sir Nicholas Poyntz at Iron Acton in Gloucestershire and Sir William Sandys at the Vyne in Hampshire, and reached its zenith with Henry Howard, Earl of Surrey, who built a sumptuous Italianate mansion at Mount Surrey on a hill outside Norwich.

By contrast Edward VI's reign saw an abrupt decline in investment in royal buildings and artefacts because of the fiscal crisis caused by war and currency debasements. The 'preaching place' at Whitehall was rebuilt on classical lines. Otherwise, it would be courtiers, not the Crown, who rebuilt or remodelled their houses. Somerset House, built by Protector Somerset in the Strand between 1547 and 1552, was the first classical building in England that could rival a royal palace in scale. Soon the tastes and values of the Court spilled down the Strand and into the West End, where nobles and privy councillors built city mansions and townhouses, and into the country where they built from scratch a growing number of so-called 'prodigy' houses—virtuoso feats of architecture, ornately decorated and big enough to entertain the monarch and courtiers as guests, with manicured gardens, fountains, and vistas looking on to parks.

Under Philip and Mary, a reinvigoration of Court culture on classical lines might have occurred had the king stayed in England for longer. A keen patron of Titian, Philip commissioned a portrait of himself from this artist at the time of the marriage negotiations in 1553. Titian subsequently worked on the theme of Venus and Adonis for presentation to Mary, and another project was Jason and Medea, dropped when someone realized that this was a totally unsuitable subject for a gift to a foreign bride.

In Elizabeth's reign, tastes remained classical to a considerable degree, but also returned to vernacular themes linked to a revival of the ideals of chivalry. This was increasingly so in the 1570s as leading courtiers urged the queen to stand firm for the Protestant cause, a trend that accelerated after the failure of the

Anjou marriage negotiations of 1579–81, when the idea of Elizabeth as the 'Virgin Queen' came to the fore. To match the change, a variety of new iconographic and cultural forms emerged, the most distinctive being a metamorphosis whereby jousts and tournaments—which under Henry VIII had been genuine displays of military skill—were transformed into the theatrical 'tilts' staged annually at Whitehall on the queen's Accession Day (17 November). Here Protestant propaganda fused with courtly love and the chivalric and classical traditions to create the legend of Elizabeth as the 'Vestal Virgin of the Reformed Religion', worshipped by her knights on the occasion of a new quasi-religious festival.

The result was a cultural hybrid, one still visible at several mid-Elizabethan prodigy houses, notably Burghley House (Figure 13), near Stamford in Lincolnshire, the ancestral home of William Cecil. The rebuilt west façade at Burghley, finished in 1577,

13. The rebuilt west façade at Burghley House, near Stamford in Lincolnshire, finished in 1577 as part of the massive construction works undertaken by Sir William Cecil after his ennoblement as Lord Burghley in 1571

has a gatehouse with oriel windows and flanking octagonal and square towers surmounted by Italian-inspired cupolas. The roof area of the building is full of fantastical architecture, including balustrades with obelisks, plinths bearing carved fireballs and heraldic beasts, and chimneys topped with miniature castles.

After outward pomp and show came enhanced luxury and privacy within the new prodigy houses. Chief among such features was the long gallery, hung with tapestries and historical portraits, where private conversations could be conducted without constant interruption from the traffic of servants. These galleries were largely modelled on those erected by Wolsey at his houses—Henry VIII had removed a particularly fine riverside example from the cardinal's lodgings at Esher to crown the building improvements he made at Whitehall Palace.

At a lower social level, the owners of country manor houses opted for comfort by using ground-floor parlours as their sitting and dining rooms in preference to the hall. The family lived there and in the first-floor chambers, while the servants worked on both these floors and in the basement, and slept in the attics, introducing the classic 'upstairs-downstairs' division between family and servants. As an added amenity, provision of fresh-water supplies and improved sanitary arrangements reflected concerns for private and public health. 'Bathing tuns' (i.e., bathtubs) could be purchased for £1 7s. 6d. and balls of sweet-scented soap were bought for 4d. a pound.

Between *c.*1530 and *c.*1569 the average size of a yeoman's house was three rooms. After *c.*1570, prosperous yeomen might have six, seven, or eight rooms; lesser farmers might aspire to two or three rooms, as opposed to the one-room cottages common in 1500. Richer farmers would build a chamber over the open hall, replacing the open hearth with a chimney stack. Poorer people favoured ground-floor extensions: a kitchen, or second bedchamber, would be added to an existing cottage. Kitchens were often separate buildings to reduce the risk of fire. A typical late Elizabethan farmstead might be described as 'one dwelling house of three bays, one barn of three bays, one kitchen of one bay'.

Corresponding improvements were made to furnishings. The average investment in furniture, beds, tableware, and kitchenware for a small farmer before 1570 was around £7. Between 1570 and 1603 it rose to £10 10s., and by the 1620s it would climb to £17. By contrast the value of the household goods of wealthier families rose by 250 per cent between 1570 and 1610, and that of the middling ranks slightly exceeded even that high figure. Many prosperous yeomen families owned feather-beds, coverlets and bed-hangings, carpets, pewter, brass, glassware, spoons, and fine linen worth up to £80.

Painting and the visual arts

In Henry VIII's and Wolsey's time, the most valued decorative art objects were tapestries. By his commissions and acquisitions in the 1520s, Wolsey almost singlehandedly set a benchmark not only for the king to follow but also for those around him. A step-change in connoisseurship was achieved after Pope Leo X commissioned Raphael in 1515 to design a set of tapestries depicting the lives of St Peter and St Paul for the Sistine Chapel in Rome. Wolsey heard of the pope's commission and consciously modelled his own purchases and patronage on similar lines. The pope's tapestries were woven at the workshops of Pieter van Aelst in Brussels, where Wolsey made several purchases. Although many of the cardinal's 600–700 tapestry pieces were only of medium quality compared to the pope's, the customized set of the *Triumphs of Petrarch* that he ordered in *c*.1520 and which hung at Hampton Court were among some 30 in his collection that were of the finest quality.

After *c*.1530 portraits were in vogue, not least because tapestries were beyond the means of all but the wealthiest consumers. The art of painting and portraiture was transformed almost single-handedly by the two visits to England of Hans Holbein the Younger. When the painter had arrived from Basel in 1526 bearing a letter of introduction from Erasmus to Thomas More, few in England cared a jot for portraits. Everything changed after Holbein was employed to paint scenery for revels in May 1527 at Greenwich to entertain a delegation of French diplomats. After that, Holbein graduated to other work, beginning with portraits of Sir Henry Guildford and his wife, and for the More family, painting both More's portrait in oils and a life-sized family group scene on linen using water-based pigments.

After Holbein returned from Basel on his second visit, Henry VIII gave the artist a major commission to immortalize the break with Rome and to brand him as 'Supreme Head of the English Church'. The king wanted a life-sized dynastic wall fresco at Whitehall, for which part of Holbein's cartoon survives. The mural, destroyed by fire in 1698 but known from copies, was for the Privy Chamber: the inner sanctum of monarchy. Henry and Jane Seymour were depicted in front of the king's deceased parents against the backdrop of a triumphal arch. A central inscription trumpeted Henry's claim to greatness: if Henry VII, the father, it said, had brought stability to the country after the Wars of the Roses, then his son, 'born to greater things', had overthrown the pope and restored 'true religion'. Who, the inscription asked rhetorically, 'was then the greater?' (illustrated in Figure 2).

Now courtiers wanted portraits from life as never before, for Holbein (and Henry) had taught them that a sitter could win immortal fame. And after the first sales of the ex-monastic lands they could afford it. The sudden release of wealth caused the market for luxury goods and art works to boom.

Holbein had no immediate successor worthy of the name, but in Elizabeth's reign, Nicholas Hilliard, who had trained as a goldsmith, became the most influential artist on the strength of his ravishing miniatures. In his capable hands, the miniature was far more than a mere reduced version of a panel portrait. To enhance the techniques learned in the workshops of Ghent and Bruges, where the miniature was painted on fine vellum and pasted on to card, Hilliard used gold as a metal, burnishing it 'with a pretty little tooth of some ferret or stoat or other wild little beast'. Diamond effects were simulated with utter conviction: Hilliard's jewel-bedecked lockets were often worn as badges or exchanged as pledges of love. And during the long war with Spain after 1585 courtiers wore the queen's portrait in miniature or in cameo as a pledge of loyalty.

Elizabeth was a patron of Hilliard, but otherwise she spent modestly on artistic commissions. With the exception of a series of portraits she commissioned to mark the second visit of Francis, Duke of Anjou, most of the surviving images of her were commissioned as gifts by courtiers or else purchased to decorate their homes in advance of an impending visit from the queen during one of her summer progresses.

In the case of a woman ruler, the Privy Council considered it to be essential to project her in a way that inspired national unity. How artists depicted her appearance, virtue, intellectual talents, and—especially after the failure of the negotiations with Anjou—her virginity would be carefully stage-managed, often aided by artists who were Dutch refugees (and therefore Protestant). The campaign was inaugurated in 1563, when Cecil drafted a proclamation forbidding artists from drawing the queen's picture until 'some special person, that shall be by her allowed, shall have first finished a portraiture thereof'. Thereafter, all other painters or engravers were to follow the currently approved 'official' template, which according to the circumstances might figure her as the patroness of peace or honour, or as victor, pious princess, or even saint.

Of these templates, the most copied model was that of the so-called 'Darnley' portrait type with its long and angular features (c.1575).

In its iconography, it marked an effort to match Continental portrait trends and to depict the impenetrable 'mask' of majesty. Other notable portrait types include the 'Pelican' and 'Phoenix' portraits (c.1575–80), so called, respectively, after pelican or phoenix jewels which the queen wears. A more realistic approach to the features of a woman who was aging is the 'Ditchley' pattern pioneered by Marcus Gheeraerts the Younger, painted to commemorate Elizabeth's visit to the house of Sir Henry Lee (c.1592).

Inevitably as the queen aged, her portraits became more stylized. By 1592, her skin was wrinkled, she wore a wig, her teeth were bad, and she placed a perfumed silk handkerchief in her mouth before receiving visitors. And yet, her portraits still depict a highly attractive woman in middle age.

The challenge for artists was to show that time took no toll on the queen's beauty. The climax was reached in the 'Rainbow' portrait (c.1600), which followed a pattern known as the 'Mask of Youth'. An idealized Elizabeth is shown as a beautiful young woman, who holds a rainbow and so plays the role of the sun-god himself. On her sleeve is a serpent, a symbol of wisdom and intelligence. Her gown is decorated with ears and eyes, representing her privy councillors and servants who watch and listen, but do not give judgement.

Hilliard had created the 'Mask of Youth' pattern initially as a miniature in c.1590 and it was most famously reused in the so-called 'Procession' portrait attributed to Robert Peake (Figure 14), in which Elizabeth appears to be carried in a litter borne by several of her gentlemen pensioners, but is actually pushed from behind on a carefully concealed ceremonial wheelchair (c.1602). The scene contains all the elements of a Roman imperial triumph, and yet with the queen dressed in white and the gaze of all the spectators transfixed upon her, she appears also as the 'Virgin Queen', the bride of Christ and of the kingdom, who is elevated to a higher plane.

14. Elizabeth I attended in procession by her gentlemen pensioners. The painting was commissioned by Edward Somerset, Earl of Worcester, who in 1601 was appointed Master of the Horse in succession to the Earl of Essex. The gentlemen support an embroidered floral canopy over the queen, who sits on a wheeled chair

Music

Music under the Tudors was chiefly invigorated by royal and noble patronage, by the continued liturgical demands of cathedrals and their choirs, and by rapid technical and stylistic advances in harmony and part-singing. At Court, trumpeters and drummers sounded alarms, wind consorts played at meal-times, lutenists and virginalists played softly in the background in the Privy Chamber, while both wind and stringed instrumentalists accompanied the dancing after the candlelit revels or plays.

An inventory of Henry VIII's musical instruments suggests that a lavish selection was available in the Privy Chamber—lutes, clavichords, virginals, and regals (small portable organs). The Flemish lutenist, Giles Duwes, who also doubled as a royal librarian, had unlimited access to these inner apartments—among his other duties, he was appointed a French and music teacher to the king's daughter, Mary. Where organists and singers were concerned, Henry's and Wolsey's chapels rivalled each other to recruit the best performers. One of Henry's triumphant successes was to poach Dionysius Memo from St Mark's in Venice for a couple of years.

In Philip and Mary's reign, England was exposed to the intense artistry of Flemish and Spanish music, while the transformative influence of Italy came in the shape of Palestrina's motets and the settings of the Florentine madrigalists. Thomas Tallis was the finest liturgical composer at this time. An accomplished organist, he was officially designated a 'gentleman' (lay singer) of the Chapel Royal. Besides performing at special occasions, the gentlemen of the Chapel, together with the children of the Chapel, sang the normal round of daily liturgical services on a rota basis.

Despite the new religious settlement of 1559, the Catholic Tallis was able to keep his post, since Elizabeth retained the music for her chapel services very much as it had been in the closing years of her father's reign. While she was queen, it was still possible for the chapel composers to set to music passages from the old Latin mass. In consequence, she was able to recruit and retain musicians and keyboard artists of the standing of William Byrd and John Bull, who secretly were Catholics.

Besides her chapel musicians, Elizabeth employed a large corps of musicians and instrument-makers from Italy, Germany, and France. Entire musical dynasties, such as the Bassanos of Venice—Jewish immigrants who had first begun to settle at her father's Court and who played wind instruments—would serve her for as long as she was on the throne. In fact, it was in secular music that some of the most startling advances were made during the final decades of the century. Byrd and his pupil, Thomas Morley, composed dozens of masterly dance settings for the virginals, including pavanes, galliards, and corantos, while Morley wrote ravishingly beautiful madrigals. By the end of the reign, they were rivalled only by another of Byrd's ex-students, Thomas Tomkins.

Literature

Thomas More's *Utopia* made his name famous as far and wide as France, Italy, and Germany—but he wrote it in Latin. His vernacular prose style could be dense and repetitive. At best, he told 'merry tales' in the style of Chaucer, many of them bawdy, inserting them liberally throughout his polemical works against heresy to hold the reader's attention.

The breakthrough came with the vernacular writings of William Tyndale and notably his translation of the *New Testament*. When these books appeared, Tyndale was rebuked for his 'rude' (i.e., simple, unornamented) and 'unclerkly' style because he wrote in a register only marginally above that of ordinary speech and used simple, often monosyllabic words to make his texts plain. His writing style greatly influenced Cranmer, and a century or so later the translators of the King James's version of the Bible largely adopted his style and often his very words.

Others preferred a more classical style when writing in the vernacular. Sir Thomas Elyot, who wrote largely in prose, published a dozen or more translations or near-translations of Latin texts, besides editing a massive Latin Dictionary in 1538. In the process, he provided a whole host of new English words for Latin terms, considerably increasing the range of vocabulary available to authors. Elyot's fascination with vocabulary accelerated in the circle around Sir John Cheke and William Cecil in Cambridge and at the Court of Edward VI. In the 1550s, Roger Ascham, Sir Thomas Hoby, and Sir Thomas Wilson were in the vanguard of a project aiming to standardize English, which (in Wilson's phrase) would become the 'King's English'.

Among poets, Sir Thomas Wyatt and Henry Howard, Earl of Surrey, transformed and rejuvenated English lyric verse after the manner of Petrarch and introduced the sonnet into England. Wyatt is the first known Englishman to translate and imitate Petrarch's sonnets and *canzone*. One of the most accomplished of the 'poets-as-lovers' or 'lovers-as-poets' who amused himself at Henry VIII's Court in 'pastime' or games of courtly love while Anne Boleyn was queen, he found himself privy to inconvenient secrets, perpetuating in verse what he tried to forget in real life.

On the more technical side, the Earl of Surrey pioneered the replacement of the old Chaucerian system of versification with something more rigorously metrical and so easier to recite without worries over the correct pronunciation of the words. But it was left to Sir Philip Sidney and Edmund Spenser to complete the process in the 1570s and 1580s. In particular, Spenser's ability to blend a variety of regional dialects in his verses without causing the reader to stumble over the words allowed subtle modulations and changes of diction and mood not possible earlier.

Spenser's masterpiece was *The Faerie Queene* (1589–90 and 1596), an epic poem examining on a dazzling multiplicity of levels the nature and quality of the late Elizabethan polity. A hybrid of elements of Italian romance, classical epic, and vernacular styles, the work is, above all, a political allegory. As the poet explained in a dedicatory epistle to Sir Walter Ralegh, 'In that Fairy Queen I mean glory in my general intention, but in my particular I conceive the most excellent and glorious person of our sovereign the Queen, and her kingdom in Fairy land. And yet, in some places else, I do otherwise shadow her.'

A contemporary reader attests to the popularity of *The Faerie Queene*, saying that the book 'was so well liked that Her Majesty gave [Spenser] a hundred marks pension forth of the Exchequer, and so clerkly was it penned, that he beareth the name of Poet Laureate'. But much of this is hyperbole, for although Elizabeth did grant Spenser an audience and a pension for life of £50 a year, it was also plain that the poet was layering his celebration of the queen with a thinly veiled critique of the ambition, corruption, intrigue, and cultural claustrophobia of the 'delightful land of Faerie', indicating that all was not quite what it seemed to be.

Unlike Spenser, the supreme literary talent of the Elizabethan age, William Shakespeare, won fame and fortune in his own lifetime. Author of 38 plays and of 154 sonnets, together with poems entitled *Venus and Adonis* and *The Rape of Lucrece*, he has exerted greater influence on literature and drama worldwide than any other individual writer in history. *Venus and Adonis* proved that he could write elegant poetry despite having no more than a standard grammar-school education. In the plays, his genius is to show audiences how to strip away the divinity of kings and force us to consider the differences between 'true' and 'false' nobility, doing so without falling prey to censorship or retribution in his own lifetime.

Of the many influences on his life and career, his Warwickshire origins were perhaps supreme. As the grandson of a yeoman farmer and the son of a failing Stratford-on-Avon shopkeeper, Shakespeare belonged to the country, not the city. He had an encyclopaedic knowledge of country lore and the medicinal uses of plants, more than enough to baffle the London typesetters who later set his plays into print.

When Shakespeare was a boy, companies of players were already retained by nobles and privy councillors for their private entertainment and during the summer months they would travel the countryside playing to audiences wherever they could be found. From the time that Thomas More's brother-in-law, John Rastell, opened the first public theatre in Finsbury Fields in London in *c.*1525, the capital became the busiest city for theatre. Elizabeth took a keen personal interest in drama, and plays were a notable feature of the Christmas and New Year revels both at

Court and the lawyers' inns of court. In 1583, the best actors from each of the various companies were taken directly under the queen's patronage and an elite company of 'Queen's Men' formed. At that time, Shakespeare was just 19.

Once Shakespeare had arrived in London and progressed from acting in plays and doctoring scripts to writing them, he relied on a wide range of sources, reading printed texts and translations voraciously. Several of his plays such as *King Lear, Coriolanus*, and *Richard II* contain dangerously topical allusions to contemporary or near-contemporary events. The English History plays, and *Richard II* in particular, were rooted in the belief of many in the 1590s that the regicide of Mary, Queen of Scots, and the failure of Elizabeth to marry or settle the succession could lead to only one outcome: the renewal of the Wars of the Roses.

Shakespeare's experience was that of a writer at a cultural crossroads. After about 1580, European literature explored increasingly the methods of individual expression and characterization associated with modern processes of thought. Shakespeare's *Hamlet* and Christopher Marlowe's *Doctor Faustus* are among the most powerful theatrical evocations in this mode. Both dramatists were eager to pursue psychology, rather than ethics. The difference is that Faustus does not pass beyond the bounds of egotism to realize self-analysis, whereas Hamlet's introspection and self-doubts are the keystones of the action.

Late medieval philosophy had dealt with the objective appreciation of senses, natures, and truth. By the 1590s, the emphasis had shifted towards subjectivity and self-expression, paradoxically under the influence of Calvinist theology, which so stressed the inflexibility of God's predestined Word that a person's quest for grace necessarily came to depend on systematic self-scrutiny.

Marlowe and Shakespeare dominated late Elizabethan drama, although they did not monopolize it. The allegories and morality plays of the late 15th century continued to flourish, especially in such provincial towns as Norwich, Chester, Coventry, and York. But the Brave New World was in London, where a large urban market existed for culture. Here audiences flocked to the theatres, aided by the development of coaches, which enabled whole families to travel up to town from the surrounding countryside and stay for months on end, to enjoy the London 'season' and to buy the luxuries that were obtainable only there.

Chapter 8
After the Armada

The last decade

The long war against Spain and its ally, the French Catholic League, was fought in multiple theatres: chiefly in France, the Netherlands, on the Atlantic, and, latterly, in Ireland. England was several times threatened with encirclement. The physical and emotional strains at home became acute. At Court, anxiety fused with the poverty of the Crown and the competition for patronage to kindle factionalism, self-interest, and instability. In London and the countryside, xenophobia, war-weariness, and the turmoil created by rising prices, bad harvests, and outbreaks of disease— chiefly plague and influenza—encouraged stiff resistance to the Crown's fiscal and military demands. All this, in turn, triggered an authoritarian reaction from privy councillors and magistrates, for whom state security, the subversiveness of religious dissent, and the threat of popular revolts became obsessions.

A clear change of personnel colours these later years. Several leaders of the first-generation establishment died between 1588 and 1590, notably Robert Dudley, Earl of Leicester, and Sir Francis Walsingham. Both had been champions of the Dutch and the Huguenots. Their deaths altered the balance of power in the Privy Council. Dudley's death created a double vacuum: his voice had been silenced and he lacked a legitimate heir, meaning his many followers were forced to seek a new patron. Many gravitated towards his stepson, the dazzling but paranoid Robert Devereux, Earl of Essex, whose rivalry with Robert Cecil, the chief minister's second son and political heir, would soon trigger in-fighting.

By the mid-1590s, politics would be thoroughly scarred by the disruptive feud between Essex and Robert Cecil. The two rivals were both in their early 30s, but whereas Essex was tall and well-proportioned with an aristocratic bearing and lofty disposition, the younger Cecil suffered from a deformed spine and diminutive height—Elizabeth called him her 'little elf'. Essex had initially regarded Cecil as a 'friend', but had little difficulty in disparaging him once friction arose between them.

Essex promptly staked his claim to his stepfather's mantle of the European Protestant cause and within three years he had succeeded him as Elizabeth's favourite. After he was admitted to the Privy Council in 1593, he sought to build a power base at Court and in the shires—his networks soon included more than 12 deputy lieutenants in charge of the local militias. Essex also resumed a secret correspondence with James VI that he had begun in 1589—sending the Scottish king advice about how to further his campaign to succeed Elizabeth, and seeking to become his confidant in the belief that she could not live much longer.

By 1596, Essex's feud with Robert Cecil had escalated into a factional battle to dominate the Privy Council and dictate both royal policy and the succession to the throne. Moreover, this battle was as damaging as anything seen since Henry VIII's death, because Essex embellished his brand of militant Protestantism with demands that the war effort be led by generals and not by civilians. He championed a switch to an aggressive strategy in Europe and the Atlantic, whereas the Cecils' goals were purely defensive, designed to keep the power of Philip II at bay and prevent Spain from seizing control of the Channel ports or intervening in Ireland.

A patriot despite all his failings, Essex was incensed when the Cecils covertly put out peace feelers to Spain. Both sides were exhausted by the war and the Cecils saw an opportunity to end it. Essex, by contrast, believed that Spain could not be trusted to maintain a peace unless it had first been defeated on the battlefield. His fiery advocacy had the support of the Dutch and the Huguenots. But the priorities of the French Huguenot leader, Henry of Navarre, rapidly changed after the assassination of Henry III in 1589. Unable by July 1593 to win complete control of the country to which he was heir as King Henry IV without League support, he had sensationally converted to Catholicism—a move that the Cecils took as a signal that he would also make his own peace with Spain.

Elizabeth's grip on events slackened markedly in these years. As her mind and body aged, her growing inaction pushed her onto the sidelines. The war effort required strategic planning and instant reflexes. Since Elizabeth tended to dither, decisions were taken on her behalf, and for the first time she tacitly condoned this. Never before had she willingly allowed her councillors to seize the initiative, and when they did so covertly—as over the dispatch of the warrant for the execution of Mary, Queen of Scots—she had reacted furiously. The danger in the 1590s was that a disappointed councillor—such as Essex—having subverted his instructions in favour of his ambition and yet still failed, would pose a direct threat to her monarchy.

The changed environment was most visible in the Church. Archbishop John Whitgift (1583–1604) differed fundamentally in outlook from his predecessor, Grindal, whom Elizabeth had suspended. When in 1591 Whitgift presided over the prosecution in the Court of Star Chamber of Thomas Cartwright and other puritan leaders on a charge of seditious conspiracy, the elder Cecil (Figure 15) was a conspicuous and deliberate absentee.

The activities of Whitgift's underlings were challenged in the Court of Queen's Bench in 1591 by James Morice, a puritan lawyer with

15. William Cecil, Lord Burghley, in old age, clasping a pink and honeysuckle as he inspects the exotic plants and shrubs in his garden, riding a mule

connections to both the elder Cecil and the Earl of Essex. But his intervention badly backfired, producing a vindication by the common-law judges of the queen's 'imperial prerogative' (i.e., unlimited sovereignty) as 'Supreme Governor' of the Church. In a sweeping decision the judges held that a sudden raft of prosecutions that Whitgift's men were bringing in the church courts against those puritan ministers who refused to conform to the 1559 settlement could not be challenged or reviewed in the ordinary courts of justice because 'by the ancient laws of this realm this kingdom of England is an absolute empire and monarchy'. The judges' ruling greatly satisfied Elizabeth, but was a far cry from what many members of Parliament believed to be the case.

Problems of government

Crown policy in the 1590s was damaging from several viewpoints. When Henry of Navarre had converted to Catholicism in 1593, he had forever soured hopes of a European Protestant coalition. Elizabeth, shocked to the core, continued to support him, but only because a united France restored the balance of power against Spain in Europe and because his debts to the English queen would otherwise have remained unpaid. But she felt a profound sense of disillusion and despair, disappearing into her bedchamber to brood. And when Henry—with the active collusion of Robert Cecil—made a unilateral peace with Spain by the Treaty of Vervins on 2 May 1598, she found her country isolated once again and her land armies dangerously vulnerable.

Next, the English quarrelled bitterly with the Dutch over their mounting debts. The cost of the war was unprecedented: it could only be met by heavy and repeated taxation, borrowing, and sales of crown lands. Lastly, the war spread to Ireland. The Irish Reformation had failed abysmally and a series of Spanish invasions just as dangerous as the Armada were attempted there. These, combined with serious internal revolts by confederated Irish forces led by Hugh O'Neill, Earl of Tyrone, and 'Red' Hugh O'Donnell, obliged the Privy Council to think in terms of the full-scale conquest of Ireland logically induced by Henry VIII's assumption of the kingship.

Elizabeth hesitated—as well she might. At last the Earl of Essex was dispatched in 1599 with a large army. But his failure surpassed even Dudley's in the Netherlands. After he deserted his post in a last-ditch attempt to salvage his career by personal

magnetism, he was put on trial for treason and beheaded in
February 1601 for leading his faction in a desperate rebellion
through the streets of London. He was deeply implicated in
treason, since shortly after his return his supporters had urged
Lord Mountjoy, his successor in Ireland, to send him 5,000 troops
to remove 'bad instruments' around Elizabeth in a Court coup.
His death left Robert Cecil all but supreme in politics.

In Ireland, Mountjoy gradually reduced the confederated chiefs to
submission and routed a Spanish invasion force. The conquest of
Ireland was largely completed by 1603, but the results were
inherently contradictory. English dominance was confirmed, but
the very fact of conquest alienated the population and
extinguished hopes of advancing the Irish Reformation and thus
achieving cultural unity with England.

Such contradictions were not confined to Irish history. The most
obvious area of decline was that of government. Did Elizabethan
institutions succumb to decay during the war with Spain? Criticism
centres on the inadequacy of taxation, local government, and military
recruitment; the rise of corruption in central administration; the
abuse of the royal prerogative to grant lucrative 'monopolies' (or
exclusive licences) in favour of courtiers and their clients; and the
claim that the benefits of the Poor Laws were negligible in relation to
the rise in population and scale of economic distress in the 1590s.

Elizabeth certainly allowed the taxation system to decline. Not
only did the value of normal taxation fail to increase in line with
inflation despite soaring levels of government expenditure, but
yields dropped in cash terms owing to static taxpayer assessments
and widespread evasion. Tax rates became stereotyped, while the
basis of assessment became the taxpayer's unsworn declaration.
Whereas Wolsey had attempted to impose realistic tax
assessments in Henry VIII's reign, Elizabeth abandoned the effort.
The elder Cecil himself evaded tax, grumbling hypocritically in
Parliament about tax cheating while keeping his own assessment

of income static at £133 6s. 8d.—his real income was approximately £4,000 per annum (£4 million in modern values). According to one critic of the system, few taxpayers were assessed at more than one-sixth or one-tenth of their true wealth, 'and many be 20 times, some 30, and some much more worth than they be set at'.

The regime's failure to increase or maintain tax yields to fund the war effort was the biggest weakness of the late-Elizabethan state. Part of the problem was that local taxation had escalated, chiefly to cover poor relief, road and bridge repairs, and expenditure incurred for the recruitment and training of the local militia. Such musters and training, which the counties had to pay for, were expensive and forced the magistrates to levy additional rates. The counties were responsible, too, for providing stocks of parish arms and armour, for paying muster-masters, for repairing coastal forts and beacons, and for issuing troops recruited for foreign service with weapons and uniforms.

In Kent, the cost of military preparations borne by the county between 1585 and 1603 exceeded £10,000. True, a proportion of 'coat-and-conduct' money required to equip and transport troops to the nearest port was recoverable from the Exchequer, but in practice the localities met roughly three-quarters of the cost. Also, whereas merchant ships (except customarily fishing vessels) had traditionally been requisitioned from the coastal towns and shires to augment the royal navy in time of war, the Crown in the 1590s started demanding money as well as ships. When the ship money rate was then extended to inland areas such as the West Riding of Yorkshire, it aroused opposition to the point where the Crown's right to impose it was questioned.

The strain of a war economy was cumulative. Conscription became a flashpoint as 105,800 men were impressed for military service in the Netherlands, France, Portugal, and Ireland during the last 18 years of the reign. Conscription for Ireland after 1594 aroused the greatest resentment. In 1600, there was a near mutiny of Kentish cavalry at Chester as they travelled to Ulster. Pressure on the shires led to administrative breakdowns and opposition to central government's demands, while endless rain, epidemics, and ruined harvests in 1596 and 1597 caused widespread distress.

At the level of central government, rising corruption signalled a drift towards venality. The shortage of Crown patronage during the long war and the log-jam in promotion prospects encouraged a traffic in offices. Competition at Court created a 'black market' in which influence was bought and sold. Offices were overtly traded, but unlike Henry VII's sales, they rarely benefited the Crown itself. Payments were made instead to courtiers to influence the queen's choice. For a minor post £200 or so would be offered, with competitive bids of £1,000 to £4,000 taken for such lucrative offices as the Receivership of the Court of Wards or Treasurership at War. And bids were investments, since if an appointment resulted, the new incumbent would so exercise his office as to recoup his outlay plus interest.

The socio-economic crisis of the 1590s

The 1590s saw the second socio-economic crisis of the century. Crime, vagrancy, and economic misfortunes, especially the catastrophic harvest failures of 1596 and 1597, headed the immediate list of concerns. Food prices climbed higher in real terms in 1594–8 than at any time before 1615, while real wages plunged lower in 1597 than at any time between 1260 and 1950. Perhaps two-fifths of the population fell below the margin of subsistence: malnutrition reached the point of starvation in the uplands of Cumbria. Disease spread unchecked, often carried around the countryside by soldiers returning from the front in France and the Netherlands. The death rate jumped by 21 per cent in 1596–7, and by a further 5 per cent in 1597–8. Even though fewer parishes experienced crisis mortality than during the influenza epidemic of 1556–9, thousands of families were thrown onto parish relief.

Given these pressures, the key to political stability in the 1590s was the solidarity of the elite. Economic conditions accelerated a process of polarization between rich and poor, which subverted traditional perceptions of order and degree yet simultaneously fostered the values of authoritarianism and a class society. The assize judges confronted a rising tide of property crime. It was no coincidence that, when sitting alongside privy councillors in the Court of Star Chamber, they remoulded and reinterpreted the criminal law to enable minor offences against private property to be punished as serious public crimes. Increasingly property-owners of any rank or position took sides with the gentry against the rabble. Those whose grandfathers had camped with Robert Kett on Mousehold Heath in 1549 now assumed local office, settled their disputes in the law courts, and closed ranks against masterless men, domestic servants, transient workers, and urban immigrants.

In a brave attempt to find solutions, Parliament in 1598 and 1601 enacted legislation for the punishment of vagrancy, and instituted a national scheme of compulsory parish rates to relieve the aged and dependent poor. Raw materials such as wool, flax, hemp, and iron were to be purchased upon which the able-bodied unemployed could be set to work—this began the system of poor relief and local rates which remained in force until the Poor Law Amendment Act of 1834.

But the new legislation was inadequate when inflation and the rise in prices are factored into the account. The estimated cash yield of independently endowed charities for poor relief by 1600 totalled £11,700 per annum—one-quarter of 1 per cent of national income. Yet the estimated amount raised by the new statutory poor rates was even smaller. If these figures are correct, what was audible was not a bang but a whimper.

The steep economic recession was made much worse by Spain's decision in 1596 to default on its loans, a move that helped to freeze Europe's money markets for a decade. Banks failed in Antwerp, Lyons, and Genoa: legitimate trade ground almost completely to a halt. The point was soon reached where the outcry in Parliament against unprecedented levels of national and local taxation, sky-high prices, large-scale poverty, and unemployment, notably youth unemployment, posed a threat to the regime's stability. Clashes in Parliament signalled unequivocal resentment of abuses promoted by courtiers and government officials.

The critics' main target was grants of monopolies to manufacture or market certain essential foodstuffs or commodities. Some were to reward genuine patents or copyrights, but many were designed simply to corner the market for the promoters, or to grant them exclusive rights, which enabled them to demand exorbitant fees from manufacturers or tradesmen for carrying out their legitimate businesses. By 1598, monopolies had doubled the price of steel, tripled that of starch, caused that of imported glassware to rise fourfold and that of salt elevenfold. Courtiers could enforce them with impunity, since patents and monopolies rested on the royal prerogative.

When a young lawyer, William Hakewill, read out a list of monopolies in Parliament in 1601 and cried out, 'Is not bread there?', Elizabeth had personally to intervene to neutralize the attack. No longer could she hide behind her officials, no longer could she pretend that she had been 'misadvised' by others, since she had clearly presided over a corrupt system of payments to courtiers and others that netted them the vast sums they needed to build their prodigy houses. When an angry crowd of protesters surged into the main lobby of Parliament and camped there refusing to leave, she had to act. Against all her instincts, she summoned members of Parliament to Whitehall Palace and addressed them as a suppliant, delivering a speech known for ever afterwards as 'the Golden Speech'.

By talking eloquently of England's glory and of the values of liberty, duty, and freedom, she won over her audience, but beneath all the rhetoric, her speech was an unashamed defence of absolute and sacral monarchy empowered by God alone. It gave away nothing of any real substance. But for the first time in British history, a monarch had been forced to invite members of Parliament to her chief palace in order to explain herself and to account publicly for the misdeeds of her ministers and courtiers.

End of an era

After the elder Cecil's death in August 1598, the Privy Council was reduced to ten, fewer than half the number when Elizabeth had come to the throne. A memorandum was drafted for her, listing eight earls and 18 barons as candidates for the vacant positions. Yet only after 1601 did she yield and agree to make some new appointments.

The queen herself died shortly before 3 am on Thursday, 24 March 1603. She had never married and she could never bring herself to settle the succession. Whether, as some contemporaries claimed, she finally acknowledged James VI of Scotland as her rightful successor with a deathbed gesture will never be known for sure. Since, however, James was the best candidate by descent and was male, Protestant and available, he was immediately proclaimed King James I of England and Ireland. The fact that his mother was Mary, Queen of Scots, was quietly forgotten, but his accession finally achieved the dynastic union of the crowns of England and Scotland sought by Henry VIII, ending one of the main threats to England's security from within the British Isles.

James ended the war with Spain in 1604. With peace restored and the arrival in the Church of England of a new generation of university-trained Protestant ministers, two of the larger problems facing Elizabeth had seemingly been resolved. But there was little nostalgia for the old queen. Despite the crowds who thronged to see her funeral procession, most people were delighted to see her go. Only after 1618, when James seemed to offer too much credence to the Catholic powers and the Thirty Years War erupted over Europe, could Elizabeth be 'reinvented' by the new king's opponents in Parliament as a decisive ruler with keen financial acumen and an unswerving commitment to the European Protestant cause—which was hardly true.

In her own lifetime, Elizabeth created the illusion of being a strong ruler, whereas the muscle was more often provided by the elder Cecil and his allies. Sir Walter Ralegh said of her approach to policy-making, 'Her Majesty did all by halves.' That said, her judgement was shrewd—often shrewder than that of her privy councillors where the enforcement of religious conformity or where military intervention abroad were at issue. She overcame the onslaught from Spain more by allowing Philip II and the Guises to overreach themselves than through her own efforts. Above all, she had luck on her side, as had her grandfather, Henry VII.

Her main aim as queen had been to preserve her father's legacy and the power of divine-right monarchy in Church and State as far as possible, but when she failed to marry and settle the succession, she excluded her father's solutions even as she sought to uphold his ideals. In consequence, she found herself confronted by increasing demands that the ruler should become accountable to Parliament. Her greatest victory was the defeat of the Spanish Armada, and yet the regicide of Mary, Queen of Scots, affected her more. Her cousin's death on the scaffold at Fotheringhay, accomplished behind her back by her privy councillors in spite of her insistence that the death warrant should not be dispatched without her further instructions, would always rankle with her. In 1601, some months after the Earl of Essex's failed revolt, she compared herself to Richard II, whom in 1399 Henry Bolingbroke had deposed.

After her death, the monarchy would never be quite the same again.

Further reading

Primary sources

G. R. Elton (ed.), *The Tudor Constitution* (Cambridge, 2nd edn, 1982), invaluable for government and administration.

L. S. Marcus, J. Mueller, and M. B. Rose (eds), *Elizabeth I: Collected Works* (Chicago, 2000), a modern-spelling edition of Elizabeth's letters and speeches.

C. H. Williams (ed.), *English Historical Documents 1485–1558* (London, 1967), the most complete source collection.

General works

J. E. A. Dawson, *Scotland Re-formed, 1488–1587* (Edinburgh, 2007), a good general introduction.

S. G. Ellis, *Ireland in the Age of the Tudors, 1447–1603: English Expansion and the End of Gaelic Rule* (London, 1998), an excellent survey.

J. Guy, *Tudor England* (Oxford, 1988), a comprehensive synthesis.

C. Haigh, *English Reformations: Religion, Politics, and Society under the Tudors* (Oxford, 1993), the leading revisionist account.

P. Williams, *The Later Tudors: England, 1547–1603* (Oxford, 1995), a detailed overview of the second half of the period.

K. Wrightson, *Earthly Necessities: Economic Lives in Early-Modern Britain, 1470–1750* (London, 2002), socio-economic history with a human face, highly readable.

Biographies

S. Alford, *Burghley: William Cecil at the Court of Elizabeth I* (London, 2008), a startling look not just at Elizabeth's chief minister but at his influence in the 1550s.

J. Guy, *'My Heart is My Own': The Life of Mary Queen of Scots* (London, 2004), focusing especially on cross-border subterfuge and the triangulation of politics between William Cecil, Elizabeth, and Mary.

C. Haigh, *Elizabeth I* (2nd edn, Harlow, 1998), the best short revisionist life.

E. W. Ives, *The Life and Death of Anne Boleyn: The Most Happy* (Oxford, 2004), not just a life of Anne, but a guide to Henry's way of thinking as well.

Leanda de Lisle, *The Sisters who would be Queen: The Tragedy of Katherine, Mary and Lady Jane Grey* (London, 2008), readable and up to date.

J. Loach, *Edward VI* (London, 1999), a useful short study.

D. MacCulloch, *Thomas Cranmer: A Life* (London, 1996), an outstanding life, full of insights especially into Edward VI's reign.

T. Penn, *Winter King: The Dawn of Tudor England* (London, 2011), conveys thrillingly the dark side of Henry VII's character.

J. M. Richards, *Mary Tudor* (London, 2008), an excellent short life aimed at students.

J. J. Scarisbrick, *Henry VIII* (London, 1968), a classic biography, still as lively and fresh as ever.

A. Somerset, *Elizabeth I* (London, 1991), a highly readable life: accurate and informative.

D. Starkey, *Henry: Virtuous Prince* (London, 2008), the early life of Henry VIII, but also a political history of Henry VII's reign.

L. Wooding, *Henry VIII* (London, 2008), the most useful life for students.

Studies of special topics

Simon Adams, *Leicester and the Court: Essays in Elizabethan Politics* (Manchester, 2002), reprints of landmark journal articles.

J. Bate, *Soul of the Age: The Life, Mind and World of William Shakespeare* (London, 2008), an exhilarating tour of the intellectual and cultural world that shaped and informed Shakespeare's thinking.

The Tudors

P. Collinson, *The Elizabethan Puritan Movement* (London, 1967), a virtuoso study of the Protestant dilemma after the 1559 settlement.

S. Doran, *Monarchy and Matrimony: The Courtships of Elizabeth I* (London, 1996), an excellent analytical account of Elizabeth's matrimonial diplomacy.

E. Duffy, *The Stripping of the Altars: Traditional Religion in England, 1400–1580* (London, 1992), includes an evocative account of the Catholic liturgical tradition on the eve of the Reformation.

E. Duffy, *Fires of Faith: Catholic England under Mary Tudor* (London, 2009), argues that England under Mary was the closest thing in Europe to a laboratory experiment for the Counter-Reformation.

G. R. Elton, *Policy and Police: The Enforcement of the Reformation in the Age of Thomas Cromwell* (Cambridge, 1972), the authoritative study of Cromwell's role in the break with Rome.

S. Gunn and P. Lindley (eds), *Cardinal Wolsey: Church, State and Art* (Cambridge, 1991), especially good on art and buildings.

J. Guy, *The Children of Henry VIII* (Oxford, 2013), shows how their childhoods and educations shaped their lives and how their interrelationships were often scarred by jealousy, mutual distrust, sibling rivalry, even hatred.

H. Hackett, *Virgin Mother, Maiden Queen: Elizabeth I and the Cult of the Virgin Mary* (London, 1994), a forensic study of the legends that circumscribe Elizabeth.

C. Levin, *The Heart and Stomach of a King: Elizabeth I and the Politics of Sex and Power* (Philadelphia, 1994), a reassessment of gender in politics.

R. Rex, *Henry VIII and the English Reformation* (London, 1993), excellent for students.

K. M. Sharpe, *Selling the Tudor Monarchy: Authority and Image in Sixteenth-Century England* (London, 2009), a comprehensive account of art and iconography.

D. R. Starkey, *Six Wives: The Queens of Henry VIII* (London, 2004), a dramatic, discriminating account of Court politics.

L. Stone, *The Crisis of the Aristocracy* (Oxford, 1965), still the most important (if controversial) study of high society.

S. Thurley, *The Royal Palaces of Tudor England: Architecture and Court Life, 1460–1547* (London, 1993), an excellent illustrated survey.

A. Walsham, *Church Papists: Catholicism, Conformity and Confessional Polemic in Early Modern England* (Woodbridge, 1993), a path-breaking academic study.

Websites

Institute of Historical Research, University of London: <www.ihr.sas.ac.uk>
Folger Shakespeare Library, Washington, DC: <www.folger.edu>
Author: <www.johnguy.com, www.tudors.org>

Chronology

1535	Executions of More, Fisher, and the leaders of the Carthusians
1536	Suppression of the Monasteries begins; revolts in Lincolnshire and Yorkshire convulse northern England
1540	Thomas Cromwell executed on charges of treason and heresy
1541	Henry VIII takes the title of King of Ireland
1542	Defeat of the Scots at battle of Solway Moss; death of James V of Scotland
1543	Treaty of Greenwich between England and Scotland
1544	Henry VIII begins 'Rough Wooing' of Scotland; war with France; English capture of Boulogne
1547	Succession of Edward VI; ascendancy of Protector Somerset; English invasion of Scotland
1548	Mary, Queen of Scots, sent to France
1549	First Book of Common Prayer; Earl of Warwick's putsch
1552	Second Book of Common Prayer
1553	Edward VI's 'Device' for the Succession; Lady Jane Grey proclaimed queen of England; Mary's counter-coup and accession
1554	Wyatt's rebellion; Jane Grey executed; Mary marries Philip of Spain; Cardinal Pole returns; reunion with Rome begins
1555	Persecution of Protestants begins
1556	Influenza epidemic begins
1557	War with France
1558	John Knox's *First Blast of the Trumpet against the Monstrous Regiment of Women* published; Mary, Queen of Scots, marries the Dauphin; accession of Elizabeth I
1559	Religious Settlement; revolt of the Protestant Lords of the Congregation in Scotland
1560	Francis II of France, husband of Mary, Queen of Scots, dies
1561	Mary, Queen of Scots, returns home
1566	Archbishop Parker's *Advertisements* demand religious conformity
1565	Mary, Queen of Scots, marries Henry, Lord Darnley
1566	Birth of James VI of Scotland (the future James I of England and Ireland)
1567	Darnley assassinated at Kirk o'Field; Mary marries James Hepburn, Earl of Bothwell; Mary forced to abdicate
1568	Mary, Queen of Scots, flees to England

1569	Northern Rising
1570	Papal bull declares Elizabeth excommunicated and deposed
1572	Treaty of Blois with France
1575	A Dutch delegation offers Elizabeth the sovereignty of Holland and Zeeland
1580	Jesuit mission to England begins
1584	William of Orange assassinated; Bond of Association
1585	Military intervention in the Netherlands led by Robert Dudley, Earl of Leicester; war with Spain
1586	Babington plot; trial of Mary, Queen of Scots
1587	Execution of Mary, Queen of Scots
1588	Defeat of the Spanish Armada
1593	Henry of Navarre converts to Catholicism
1594	Bad harvests begin, worst in 1596 and 1597; Nine Years' War begins in Ireland
1598	Henry IV of France makes a unilateral peace with Spain
1601	Earl of Essex's rebellion
1603	Death of Elizabeth; accession of James VI of Scotland as James I; peace in Ireland

Index

THE REFORMATION
A Very Short Introduction
Peter Marshall

The Reformation transformed Europe, and left an indelible mark on the modern world. It began as an argument about what Christians needed to do to be saved, but rapidly engulfed society in a series of fundamental changes. This *Very Short Introduction* provides a lively and up-to-date guide to the process. Peter Marshall argues that the Reformation was not a solely European phenomenon, but that varieties of faith exported from Europe transformed Christianity into a truly world religion. It explains doctrinal debates in a clear and non-technical way, but is equally concerned to demonstrate the effects the Reformation had on politics, society, art, and minorities.

www.oup.com/vsi

AFRICAN HISTORY
A Very Short Introduction
John Parker & Richard Rathbone

Essential reading for anyone interested in the African continent and the diversity of human history, this *Very Short Introduction* looks at Africa's past and reflects on the changing ways it has been imagined and represented. Key themes in current thinking about Africa's history are illustrated with a range of fascinating historical examples, drawn from over 5 millennia across this vast continent.

'A very well informed and sharply stated historiography . . . should be in every historiography student's kitbag. A tour de force . . . it made me think a great deal.'

Terence Ranger,
The Bulletin of the School of Oriental and African Studies

www.oup.com/vsi

THE FIRST WORLD WAR

A Very Short Introduction
Michael Howard

By the time the First World War ended in 1918, eight million people had died in what had been perhaps the most apocalyptic episode the world had known. This *Very Short Introduction* provides a concise and insightful history of the 'Great War', focusing on why it happened, how it was fought, and why it had the consequences it did. It examines the state of Europe in 1914 and the outbreak of war; the onset of attrition and crisis; the role of the US; the collapse of Russia; and the weakening and eventual surrender of the Central Powers. Looking at the historical controversies surrounding the causes and conduct of war, Michael Howard also describes how peace was ultimately made, and the potent legacy of resentment left to Germany.

'succinct, comprehensive and beautifully written. Indeed reading it is an experience comparable to scanning the clues of a well-composed crossword puzzle. Every allusion is eventually supplied with an answer, and the finished product defies the puzzler's disbelief that the intricacies can be brought to a convincing conclusion. . . . Michael Howard is the master of the short book'

TLS

www.oup.com/vsi

Islamic History
A Very Short Introduction
Adam J. Silverstein

Does history matter? This book argues not that history matters, but that Islamic history does. This *Very Short Introduction* introduces the story of Islamic history; the controversies surrounding its study; and the significance that it holds - for Muslims and for non-Muslims alike. Opening with a lucid overview of the rise and spread of Islam, from the seventh to twenty first century, the book charts the evolution of what was originally a small, localised community of believers into an international religion with over a billion adherents. Chapters are also dedicated to the peoples - Arabs, Persians, and Turks - who shaped Islamic history, and to three representative institutions - the mosque, jihad, and the caliphate - that highlight Islam's diversity over time.

'The book is extremely lucid, readable, sensibly organised, and wears its considerable learning, as they say, 'lightly'.'

BBC History Magazine

www.oup.com/vsi

MARTIN LUTHER
A Very Short Introduction
Scott H. Hendrix

This introduction presents Martin Luther as historians now
see him. Instead of singling him out as a modern hero,
the book emphasizes the context in which Luther worked,
the colleagues who supported him, and the opponents who
adamantly opposed his agenda for change. Scott H. Hendrix
explains the religious reformation and Luther's importance,
without ignoring the political and cultural forces that led
the reformation down paths Luther could neither foresee nor
influence. This *Very Short Introduction* pays tribute to Luther's
genius, but also recognizes the self-righteous attitude
that alienated contemporaries, offering a unique explanation
for that behaviour.

www.oup.com/vsi

WITCHCRAFT
A Very Short Introduction
Malcolm Gaskill

Witchcraft is a subject that fascinates us all, and everyone knows what a witch is - or do they? From childhood most of us develop a sense of the mysterious, malign person, usually an old woman. Historically, too, we recognize witch-hunting as a feature of pre-modern societies. But why do witches still feature so heavily in our cultures and consciousness? From Halloween to superstitions, and literary references such as Faust and even Harry Potter, witches still feature heavily in our society. In this Very Short Introduction Malcolm Gaskill challenges all of this, and argues that what we think we know is, in fact, wrong.

> 'Each chapter in this small but perfectly-formed book could be the jumping-off point for a year's stimulating reading. Buy it now.'
>
> **Fortean Times**

SOCIAL MEDIA
Very Short Introduction

Join our community
www.oup.com/vsi

- Join us online at the official Very Short Introductions **Facebook** page.
- Access the thoughts and musings of our authors with our online **blog**.
- Sign up for our monthly **e-newsletter** to receive information on all new titles publishing that month.
- Browse the full range of Very Short Introductions online.
- Read **extracts** from the Introductions for free.
- Visit our library of **Reading Guides**. These guides, written by our expert authors will help you to question again, why you think what you think.
- If you are a teacher or lecturer you can order inspection copies quickly and simply via our website.